#MAXIMUMFLAVOR
SOCIAL

FOOD, FAMILY & FOLLOWERS

Published by Maximum Flavor, Inc.

ISBN 978-0-9909716-2-7

First Printing 2014
Copyright Maximum Flavor, Inc. © 2014
All rights reserved

Author: Adrianne Calvo
With Juan Carlos Blanco
Executive Producer: Michael Beovides
Photography courtesy of Ines Ayra
Proofreader: Victoria Labarta
Design by: Erick Coego

Printed in the Unites States

Publisher's Note
The recipes contained in this book are to be followed exactly as written. The publisher is not responsible for your spe-cific health or allergy needs that may require medical supervision. The publisher is not responsible for any adverse reac-tions to the recipes contained in this book.
Publisher does not have any control over and does not assume any responsibility for author or third-party
Web sites on their content.

facebook.com/chefadrianne
twitter.com/chefadrianne
instagram.com/chefadrianne
chefadriannes.com
adriannecalvo.com
makeitcountcharities.org

Often times flavor
Can define you.

- Chef Adrianne

I dedicate this book to my family and to all those who believed in me every step of the way. I thank God every day for giving me the blessing of sharing my craft with the world and for providing me with an amazing team to execute my craziness. With a humble heart, I thank you. Thank you. Thank you. Thank you.

#CONTENTS

#INTRO

TWEET BEFORE (YOU) EAT

In an age where social media has taken what we choose to share to an unprecedented level, the early bird not only gets the worm, he also shows everyone how tantalizing it looks, tells them how good it tastes, and lets them know the spot he got it from is totally the IT PLACE! These days, those 4 simple words drive home the point that what we consume feeds and sustains both our bodies and our insatiable need to socialize and connect with others.

As I hope you will come to know, I'm not the type of person that goes around finding ways to insert a quote into a conversation, unless there is no better way to communicate what I mean or feel. With that being said, I've always found a simple but very accurate observation from one of the great philosophers to really resonate with me:

"Man is by nature a social animal" - Aristotle

I would have liked to have added "and woman" to that quote but that's a subject for a whole other book! It does seem however, as if we, man or woman, gain a large part of our identity from our relationship to others, building a substantial part of our character from the countless moments we share with family, friends, and colleagues over time.

Personally, I have always found that sitting down to grab a bite with others, whether that meal is in the company of a special someone or shared with a loud crowd of 20, is the perfect representation of how eminent social interaction is in all of our lives. Growing up in a Cuban household, I can tell you that we were never at a loss for words, or thankfully, food! As with most families, we were always on-the-go. It was really at dinner time in particular when we could all pause and sit still long enough to talk to each other, laugh, and just enjoy the company of one another. From the outside looking in, I'm sure it often looked like a scene out of the hilarious sitcom "Que Pasa USA?", but it's those unique connections that we build in situations where we are bonding with others that make social interaction so fascinating.

Both professionally and personally, I've seen history repeat itself in my adult years. I've observed that same type of "social magic" produced when there's at least two people gathered around a table. I've been witness to special occasions being commemorated, accomplishments big or small being celebrated, as well as major decisions being reached over quite a few lunches and dinners. And sometimes, I've also seen a meal simply serve as a backdrop for some much needed private, uninterrupted time.

The blissful feeling that these types of situations can produce has inspired me to try to capture that same sublime connection between food and the forging of social bonds for my guests at Chef Adrianne's. My goal is for each of my guests to be fully immersed in all of the social aspects that are part of preparing, consuming, and experiencing a meal. I want them to feel a tangible connection to the vines in Wine Country, the hands that passionately prepared their food, the artist that gave life to the paintings on the walls, and to the musicians that composed the music they are listening to– it is this type of connection that confirms our humanity and connection to life and each other.

So if a meal holds so much positive potential face-to-face, what happens when you can also share that experience with as many of your virtual "peeps" as possible, wherever they might be? The reach of the digital universe is positively insane, and how that has manifested itself and revolutionized the way we have come to prepare, present, savor, and even celebrate our food is one of the main themes of this book.

We live in an age where whetting the appetite of a potential guest with a tempting photograph of what's on the menu is as easy as letting your smart phone camera, paired with the power of Facebook, Twitter, and Instagram go to work! And from the perspective of the consumer, a little "virtual gloating" to your circle about the explosion of deliciousness you just experienced at your favorite lunch or dinner spot is never more than a few taps away. At Chef Adrianne's, we've truly seen these forums bring a whole new dimension to our dishes, the way they're enjoyed, and the awareness and anticipation surrounding them.

This incredible synergy between the primal social influence of food, digital, and Chef Adrianne's "worlds" is the driving force behind what lies in the pages ahead. After witnessing this energy that has led to so many memorable moments each day, both "on screen" and in the confines of the restaurant, I felt driven to capture some of the many snapshots that have often amazed, humbled, and delighted me. I invite you to enjoy a detailed look at how our newest ways of communicating have influenced and helped guide my life's passion – cooking.

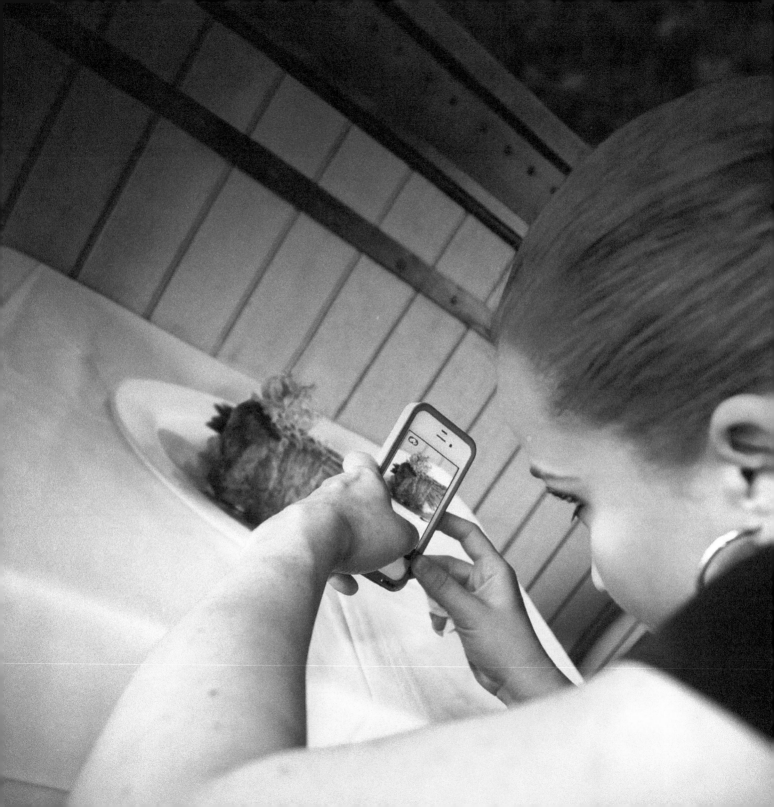

GROWING UP CALVO

You may have noticed that there's usually a clue in many people's lives in the form of a childhood incident or photo that foreshadows what they will eventually be passionate about. Looking back, I guess it should have been obvious that I was destined for the culinary life when you consider two of my earliest epic "Throwback Thursday"-type pics involve food! In one, I was caught trying to sneak a lick of the tip of a delicious flan prepared by my mother on Christmas Eve. The second one happened to be a classic rite of passage back in my day, the infamous Sears child portrait. On that memorable occasion, only a lady finger could get me to be civil long enough for the photographer to do his thing. When you factor in that a trip to the toy store for me meant blowing by all the Barbie dolls and heading straight for the toy kitchen accessories and the legendary E-Z Bake Oven, it was clear that I had many long but totally awesome days and nights inside the kitchen in my future!

I'm proud to be able to say that "growing up Calvo" was truly a great experience, and not just for the corny reasons you might expect. Don't get me wrong, my parents definitely gave us tons of love and support growing up. But had you asked me then, I would have told you that for me home was not only "where the heart is", but where you could always find loads of crazy good food too! A successful salon owner who was Expert Hairdresser by day, my mom was totally transformed into Master Chef by night, turning dinner time at the Calvo household into a daily celebration complete with a tantalizing dessert to top it all off. In fact, I'm not sure how much work my dad really got done the last couple of hours each day, because I imagine as the clock ticked away his mind was more focused on what was on the menu that night than anything else. My mom's prowess in the kitchen preceded her to the extent that on most afternoons, my dad's briefcase had barely hit the ground before he was making a beeline from the front door to see what the night's "special" was!

Although I don't have any picture perfect childhood scenes of learning my way around the kitchen at my mom's side, she definitely modeled the beauty of the detail that goes into cooking a meal from scratch. I spent plenty of afternoons with her in grocery store aisles, watching her be as selective as possible in picking the freshest ingredients she could for her next culinary work of art. Simply by keeping my ears open as she looked over different items, I definitely picked up countless major and minor details of what can really make or break certain dishes.

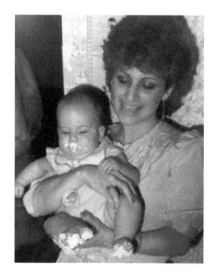

Through observing the sheer joy that was associated with sharing a meal in my childhood home, it really sunk in that dinner time was a daily event meant to be celebrated and thoroughly enjoyed. Not only did I take note of the time and effort that went into the entire meal, I also couldn't help notice the major props the cook got for pleasing our palates every single time! This whole routine of putting some heart, soul, care, and attention into making something delicious, serving it to a waiting audience, and then soaking in the accolades really started to resonate nicely with me!

As is usually the case with a true life passion, my obsession with all things food continued to grow as I did. In my middle school years, while a lot of my friends were spending the afternoon catching the latest scandal on Jerry Springer, I would take over the TV and immerse myself into some of the earliest cooking shows on the Food Network. My grandparents' guilty pleasures, their "novelas", never stood a chance! Like the devoted family members of other kids who have very strong interests from an early age, my poor "abuelos" did not escape my OCD for the kitchen. They were nice enough to humor me as I gave them a detailed play-by-play account of what was being prepared on each day's episode and tried my best to convince them how absolutely fascinating all of it really was! In a sense, this daily routine way back when had its own bit of foreshadowing. Without fully realizing it, I was already making my future career a family and social affair by sharing my enthusiasm with them on a daily basis. Years later, my immediate family would prove to a have a crucial role in the development and ongoing success of Chef Adrianne's.

Mind you, this would not have been easy to imagine during those years. When I announced my intention to bypass a traditional 4 year college to go the route of attending a reputable culinary school following high school graduation, it wasn't exactly met with overwhelming enthusiasm. As I said before, my parents have always strived to be a great support system, but I'd be lying if I said they didn't have a healthy amount of skepticism at the thought of me trying to forge a career as a chef. In fact, the idea of a female executive chef was something completely unrealistic to my dad in particular, and I have to admit his doubts were pretty valid at the time. There was not really any precedent for a woman reaching that status in a kitchen, so initially he assumed the highest I was getting on the totem pole was somewhere less than the top.

It took a personal visit to my alma mater Johnson and Wales University for both my parents to be sold on this whole crazy "food thing" for their daughter! The school, one of the very best of its kind in the country, did an awesome job of wowing them and getting them on board with my vision of what I was hoping to accomplish. Having grown up in a close knit family, there was no doubt that any professional goal that I could reach was going to be that much sweeter if those closest to me were by my side cheering me on.

I consider myself very lucky to be able to say that my both of my great loves-food and family-are totally interconnected and intertwined in my life to this day. I would never have it any other way! As a matter of fact, it's no exaggeration to say that I've had the unwavering support of my parents from the very first moment I started to even dare to dream of what would become Chef Adrianne's: My dad was my advance "scout" when I took an interest in checking out a location or two after starting to conjure up the idea of opening up my own restaurant; my mom was with me the day I spotted a Latin cafeteria in its final days at the corner of a small strip shopping plaza and somehow pictured it as a perfect spot to open what I hoped would be a Napa Valley-inspired restaurant and wine bar!

These days, Mom is my "Swiss Army Knife", helping with any errands, showing off her artistic/creative flair as the restaurant's designer for each of our uniquely themed, insanely popular Dark Dining events, and even taking it back to the old school from time to time by displaying her skills as the original Calvo Master Chef! Dad is our resident "Mr. Fix-It", insuring there are no hiccups throughout our hectic days and wonderfully crazy nights. And last but certainly not least, my dear hubby is the "Mad Scientist" behind the bar, and the guilty party responsible for some wickedly outrageous watermelon mojitos (among many other refreshing beverages) that have had our guests buzzing in more ways than one in recent times!

All in all, considering the pattern of togetherness through food that has seemingly followed me my entire life, it's no surprise that going to "work" each day truly feels like home in every sense and aspect! It's this same sense of family and social bonding that we strive to manifest each day at Chef Adrianne's through our ambiance, food, and our own unique connections to each other.

#cuban pork roast

1 large 4 or 5 pound pork roast shoulder
2 cups sour orange or fresh lime juice
1 large bay leaf
2 teaspoon dried oregano
2 teaspoon cumin, ground
2 tablespoon kosher salt
½ teaspoon black pepper
20 clove garlic peeled, cloves can be left whole
    cuban mojo sauce
2 large onions sliced in thin rounds
½ cup roast pork pan drippings
½ cup reserved garlic and lime sauce mixture

Take your pork shoulder and stab it all over making deep slits in the meat. Next take your salt pour about two tablespoons full in your hands and rub deep all over the pork roast sticking your fingers in the slits to salt the meat well.

CUBAN MOJO :
In a blender add sour orange juice, garlic cloves, and the seasonings bay leaf, cumin, oregano, pepper, 1 teaspoon salt. Blend on high until all is blended. Pour one cup of the mojo in a jar cover and reserve for later. Now take your pork roast and pour the rest of the sauce all over the pork roast rubbing the mojo sauce deep into the pork meat in the slits. When done, sprinkle a little more oregano, cumin, black pepper over the entire roast again just a little sprinkle. Cover with aluminum foil; and refrigerate until the next day for roasting. Next day remove pork from the refrigerator let stand on the counter for at least an hour then put into a preheated 325 degree oven. Depending on how large a roast you have roast about 45 minutes per pound. Pour a half cup of the reserved mojo and baste your roast every hour with some of the mojo. Roast is done when the juices run clear and the meat is tender. Do not cover with aluminum foil to roast. When done, remove roast from the oven take out of the pan put into another pan. Let roast hang out for a bit. ***Serves 6-8***

Dad and Grandma carv the Pig on Christmas!

#black beans

1 pound black beans, washed
¼ cup extra virgin olive oil
1 large yellow onion, chopped
1 medium green bell pepper, chopped
10 cloves garlic, peeled and minced
5 cups water
3 ounces tomato paste
1 tablespoon vinegar
¼ cup dry white wine
3 bay leaves
2 teaspoons salt
1 teaspoon white sugar
1 teaspoon black pepper

Place beans in a large saucepan with enough water to cover, and soak 8 hours, or overnight; drain.

Heat oil in a medium saucepan over medium heat, and saute onion, green bell pepper, and garlic until tender. Into the onion mixture, stir the drained beans, water, tomato paste, wine, bay leaves, sugar and vinegar. Season with salt, sugar, and pepper. Bring to a boil. Cover, reduce heat, and simmer 1 ½ hours, stirring occasionally, until beans are tender. *Serves 6-8*

In culinary arts there isn't a better example of fusion and culture than this traditional dish of Cuban black beans. It's the merge of Spanish and African to make this delicious dish.

Lining up for the best beans In town!

#cuban tostones

3 to 4 cups canola oil
2   green plantains
**   salt to taste**

Pour 2-3 inches of oil into a deep-fat fryer or skillet over medium-high heat. As the oil heats, cut the ends off of each plantain, and make a slice along the length of the skin. You should be able to remove the peel in one piece. Slice each plantain into pieces about two inches long . Add the pieces to the hot oil. Set them sideways into a pan, then put them in the pan and use a spatula or tongs to stand them upright one at a time. Fry them for about two minutes until they start to get slightly golden, then flip them over, frying for another two minutes. Remove the cooked pieces from the pan, and drain them on paper towels. Let them cool for at least 1-3 minutes. Take one of the pieces, and smash it in a tostonera (tostones press).

If you don't have a tostonera, you can use wax paper and a can of food or similar heavy object. Place the plantain piece upright on wax paper, fold the wax paper over the top of it, and then smash it until it is 1/4 inch thick. You can smash it down with a can of food. The longer the plantain slice, the larger the round disc you end up with will be. Some people like small, thick rounds. Others prefer them large and flat.

Once the cooking oil is hot again, add all of the plantain slices and fry them on both sides until golden brown (about 1-3 minutes). Remove the tostones from the oil, and drain them on paper towels. Sprinkle with salt. **Serve 6**

All Muse ladies compete for best family tostones!

#cuban flan

½ cup sugar
1 teaspoon water
1 whole egg
5 egg yolks
1 (12 ounce) can evaporated milk
1 (14 ounce) can sweetened condensed milk
1 teaspoon pure vanilla extract pinch of salt

Using a casserole dish, make the caramel in a saucepan by melting over medium high heat and pouring into the bottom of the casserole dish.

As you prepare the custard, the caramel will cool. In a separate bowl, using a whisk, beat the 1 whole egg and 5 egg yolks together . Add the evaporated milk and sweetened condensed milk to the eggs and mix together. Add the vanilla extract and the pinch of salt.

Pour the custard mixture into the casserole dish over the hardened caramel. Place your flan on a baking pan and fill with hot water to about halfway up the sides. Bake in a pre-heated 350 degree oven for 45 minutes. Turn off the oven and let set for another 15 minutes. Remove from the oven and the water-bath and let cool. Run a butter-knife around the outside edge of the flan. Place a plate large enough to handle the liquid caramel over the flan and invert. Chill the flan for at least an hour before serving. **Serves 8**

Flan is a staple in every day Cuban family get together, in may family we judge a great flan by how creamy it is, it can't be too sweet or have holes (that mean it overcooked) It's an exciting moment when we get a perfect flan

In the lab with Mom

Maybe I won't get Caught

IT'S YOUR CANVAS TO PAINT WHATEVER YOU WANT ✕ ON

That awkward but totally exhilarating moment, when you realize that it's your canvas to paint whatever you want on- that sums up my feelings when it really sunk in that I had an awesome opportunity in front of me. There's always a big gap between getting direction from someone above you and actually having your name on something; when I took the leap and opened up Chef Adrianne's, I had to learn to close that gap with quickness! I realized from the jump that I had to take the lead in creating everything from scratch, and nothing was more important than the menu itself. Everything from the simplest appetizer to our featured dish every evening was going to reflect how well I could exceed my guests' expectations, and how much deliciousness I could bring them while satisfying their cravings.

In the two year period between the opening of Chef Adrianne's and my first attempt at social media , I went ahead and basically relied on word-of-mouth feedback from repeat guests to the restaurant and good old-fashioned gut instinct to map out what I wanted to offer from night to night. Around 2009, when Facebook started to become THE way to share and connect with others, I had a few friends tell me how it could be a potentially great opportunity to get the word out about what we had going on each day at the restaurant. I have to admit that at first, those suggestions pretty much fell on deaf ears. Luckily over time, more open minds prevailed and I eventually dipped my toe in the water by creating a profile that mainly focused on what was happening in my professional life.

Looking back now at my days as a "novice" in the digital world, it's funny to remember how at first I had enough trouble figuring out how to post a written response or update, never mind uploading an actual picture or video! Slowly, through a little trial and error, as well as some very valuable help, I began to feel my way around how to use my page as a platform to communicate with my steadily growing group of online friends. Then, when I finally took that first baby step towards really intersecting the social media world with my daily restaurant life, something pretty awesome started to develop! I didn't realize it at the time, but one particular little social media habit I kind of fell into really became a signature tool for me to get into the minds (and palates!) of my present and potential future guests.

Once I started to get the hang of what Facebook had to offer, giving our online followers a look ahead at what was featured on that night's menu by posting a picture became a daily tradition. At first, I was kind of taken aback by how many people had very organic and excited responses to seeing what we were planning to serve. Over time, as we received consistently positive feedback, I realized that this really wasn't that surprising after all. Food has always been a crucial part of basic human social experience and sometimes just catching a glimpse of something delicious is enough to spark loads of interest and conversation. Remember back in the day when you'd bring those cool Fruit Gushers or even that special homemade sandwich to school? Before you knew it you had old and new friends hovering around your spot at the lunch table!

Take that same natural magnetism of food , combine it with the explosive power of channels like Facebook ,Instagram, and Twitter, and you have people literally and figuratively feeding off of each other's enthusiasm and excitement! That dish that at one time would have only caught the eye of your clique is now scoped out by a potential worldwide audience, being talked about and talked up between friends, strangers, and everyone in between! From a chef's and restaurant owner's perspective, this is a full 360 from what I observed in the pre-social media world. The old school approach of posting the daily special on an easel board out front and maybe having samples sitting out for hours on end were completely limited in comparison; they simply couldn't provide the chef with that valuable insight into whether their dishes were pushing any hot buttons with their guests.

In contrast, my online dialogue and relationship with my followers and friends has really paved the way for me to push forward with confidence when I go "outside the box" with our featured dishes. The way I've always seen it, "culinary art" is the perfect term to describe what a chef strives to produce every time they're in the kitchen; just like in any other creative pursuit, you start with a blank slate and then work towards putting that which is uniquely "you" into the finished product . But while it's always a blessing to have that opportunity, that doesn't mean it comes without some uncertainty over how your vision might mesh with what your target audience- your guests- might want and like. No matter how seasoned you are in the kitchen, there's always a bit of butterfly action going on when you're putting yourself out there in the form of a new dish that's supposed to be the centerpiece of the night.

Of course, there's a lot of truth in the old adage that there is no substitute for preparation. I definitely try to give every ounce of effort into making sure I'm putting my best foot forward every time those doors of Chef Adrianne's open for business. Once our featured recipes for that night are identified, I put that crucial list of ingredients together. A trip to the market, calls, visits to other suppliers, in order to source out and eventually secure everything that it will take to hopefully make that next creation another Maximum Flavor masterpiece!

The real work begins next, as I prep and create a sample dish of that night's special for my trusty focus group that I can always count on for honest feedback- my awesome Chef Adrianne's staff and my sous chef! Our daily "taste test" is a mini social event in and of itself, with food once again being the force behind gathering everyone together. It's also during this time that the featured dish takes center stage and gets its all- important pic taken- the snapshot that opens the door for letting me know how well my instincts are clicking with my guests' culinary turn-ons. When I see my social media accounts blow up about a minute after I post one quick but very tantalizing smartphone photo of that night's special, it totally confirms I've struck a chord and am on the right track!

While on the whole topic of our specials, one question I'm often asked is about what my sources of my inspiration are for coming up with the Maximum Flavor-infused appetizers, main courses and even desserts that we serve on a nightly basis. Luckily for me, my brainstorming seemed to come from all directions! With food pretty much always on my mind, it could be a conversation I have, something I may have seen in a recent movie, a simple day dream, or just a good old fashioned jonesing for something that gets the creative juices flowing. Other times what drives me in a certain direction in the kitchen might be the motivation to completely change my perspective on something I had before that I did NOT really care for. And when it comes to admiring mouth-watering dishes that are posted by others on social media, I'm no different than any other "foodie"- I have a totally hyper-sensitive connection between my eyes and salivary glands!

#tonight
recipe index

#vineyard salad

2 **cups organic mixed field greens**
½ **cup dried cranberries**
¼ **cup maple lardons, (recipe follows)**
¼ **cup fresh pear, diced**
¼ **cup champagne vinaigrette (recipe follows)**
¼ **cup french mild goat cheese, crumbled**
¼ **cup champagne vinegar**
1 **tablespoon minced shallot**
½ **teaspoon minced garlic**
½ **teaspoon Dijon mustard**
½ **teaspoon maple syrup**
½ **teaspoon salt**
¼ **teaspoon freshly ground black pepper**
¼ **cup vegetable oil**
¼ **cup olive oil**
¼ **cup bacon, diced**
¼ **maple syrup**

Whisk together all of the ingredients in a medium sized mixing bowl until emulsified or well incorporated.

MAPLE LARDONS:
Preheat oven to 300 degrees. Mix the bacon and the maple syrup well and place on a cookie sheet. Bake for 15-25 minutes or until caramelized. Remove from cookie sheet and let cool. Can be stored for up to 5 days.

TO ASSEMBLE:
In a mixing bowl, combine mixed greens and vinaigrette. Toss to make sure the greens are dressed evenly. Place on plate, and then top with lardons, pear, cranberries, and goat cheese.
Serves 2

Really craving a #VinyardSalad from @ChefAdrianne #maximumflavor #yum #bringmesome

Its fascinating to me, to take vegetables to another level. From texture to spices, its cool to see how much more can be done other than steaming boiling and baking.

#maple and serrano chili glazed carrots
crispy kale, crispy cornbread

12 large carrots, peeled, sliced lengthwise
½ cup butter
½ cup maple syrup
½ teaspoon serrano chili, minced
   kosher salt and freshly ground black pepper
¼ cup kale, washed and patted dried
¼ cup cornbread, store-bought

Preheat the oven to 250 degrees F.

Line a cookie sheet with kale leaves. Bake unit crispy, like a chip. About 5-7 minutes. In a food processor, pulse corn bread to make crumbs. Place corn bread crumbs on a cookie sheet and bake for 10 minutes. Melt butter in a large heavy sauté pan over medium-low heat.
Add carrots, cover, and cook, stirring occasionally, until carrots are fork-tender, 25–30 minutes. Increase heat to medium high, and stir in syrup and Serrano chili.
Cook for 3-4 minutes, then season to taste with salt and pepper. To assemble, place caramelized carrots on a serving dish.
Top the carrots with corn bread crumbs and crispy kale chips. Add extra maple chili glaze from the pan onto the serving dish. *Serves 4*

#charred brussel sprouts
sweet soy, garlic, truffle

1 **pound brussel sprouts, cleaned and rinsed, stems removed**
½ **cup butter, melted**
¼ **cup garlic, minced**
¼ **cup light sweet soy sauce**
1 **teaspoon white truffle oil**
   parmesan shavings
   freshly ground black pepper

Preheat the oven to 400 degrees F.

In a mixing bowl, toss brussel sprouts in butter, garlic, and soy. Place on a baking sheet and bake for 7-10 minutes or just until brussel leaves begin to crisp up and char.

Place on a serving dish and drizzle with white truffle oil, Parmesan shavings, and sprinkle freshly ground pepper on top to taste. ***Serves 4***

I know brussel sprouts are on every hip restaurant menu nowadays, so I thought why not share this super easy and delicious recipe for them.

My favorite corn on this planet. As I'm writing this I can't help but stare at this pic.

#roasted corn chip corn
queso blanco, lime, chives

4 ears corn, silks removed but the husks left on
½ cup butter, unsalted
1 cup queso blanco, finely crumbled
1 cup corn chips, finely pulverized
½ cup chives, minced
1 lime, quartered lengthwise
   chipotle hot sauce, optional

Preheat the oven to 400 degrees F.
Rub corn with butter all over. Place on a baking sheet and roast for 15-20 minutes or until corn kernels begin to separate and caramelize. Cut each corn into 4 pieces.
Top each piece with a heaping spoon of queso blanco, then top with pulverized corn chips. Add chives and garnish with a lime wedge and chipotle hot sauce. **Serves 4**

Like   Comment

Chef Adrianne Calvo
Tonight's Crispy Homestead Corn + Cojita Cheese + Powdered Fritos + Lime and Chipotle at Chef Adrianne's!!
www.chefadriannes.com
Like · Comment · Share · June 27, 2012

👍 19 people like this.

🔁 2 shares

Interesting!!:0)
June 27, 2012 at 9:22pm · Like

oishii ne... 😊

#steamed pork buns
sweet soy, garlic chili sauce

5 cups all purpose flour, plus 1/3 cup

2/3 cup water

1 1/3 cup milk, divided

1/3 cup sugar

1 teaspoon salt

4 teaspoons instant yeast

2 eggs

4 tablespoons melted butter

egg wash (1 egg, beaten with a tablespoon of milk)

FOR THE FILLING:

2 tablespoons canola oil

½ cup red onion, minced

2 tablespoons sugar

1 ½ tablespoons light soy sauce

2 tablespoons oyster sauce

1 ½ tablespoon sesame oil

1 tablespoon dark soy sauce

¾ cup chicken stock

3 tablespoons flour

2 cups diced chinese roast pork (cha siu)

sweet soy sauce

garlic chili paste

In a medium saucepan, mix 1/3 cup flour with water and 1/3 cup milk until the flour is dissolved.

Cook over medium heat and stir constantly until the mixture becomes a thick paste, about 3-5 minutes then set aside.

In a large mixing bowl, combine 5 cups of flour, sugar, salt, and yeast. Add the flour paste, 1 cup milk, 2 eggs, and melted butter. Stir together to form a dough, and knead for 15-20 minutes. You can do this by hand or in an electric mixer with a dough hook.

Form the dough into a ball and place into a lightly greased bowl. Cover with a damp cloth, and let rise for 1 hour. Meanwhile, make the meat filling. Heat 2 tablespoons oil in a wok or sauté pan, over medium high heat. Add the onion and stir-fry for 2 minutes. Add the sugar, soy sauce, oyster sauce, sesame oil, and dark soy.

Stir and cook until it starts to bubble up. Add the chicken stock and flour. Reduce the heat to medium low and cook, stirring, for 2-3 minutes until thickened. Remove from the heat and stir in the roast pork. Set aside to cool. After it has risen, separate the dough into 16 equal pieces. Shape each piece into a small circle, where the center is a bit thicker than the edges. Fill each with meat filling, and crimp them closed, making sure they're tightly sealed. Lay them out seam side down on baking sheets lined with parchment paper, and let rise for another hour. Preheat the oven to 400 degrees F.

Brush with egg wash. Put them in the oven and immediately turn the oven down from 400 degrees to 325 degrees. Bake for about 25 minutes, or until golden brown. To serve, spoon sweet soy sauce and garlic chili paste on the plate and place 4 buns on each plate. **Serves 4**

The texture of
these buns are
unique and become
addictive

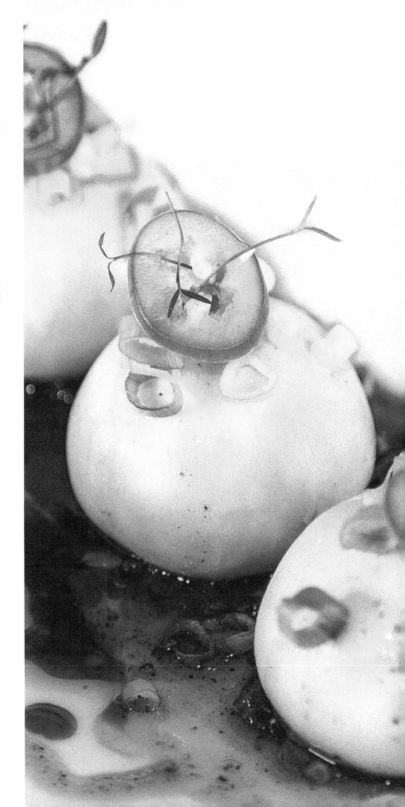

This is one of the
first recipes I made
on my segment on
NBC 6.

#fried avocado
spicy salsa cream

2 **cups vegetable oil**
2 **avocados, halved, seeded, peeled and**
   sliced lengthwise
   kosher salt
½ **cup all-purpose flour**
1 **large egg, beaten**
1 **cup cornmeal**

SPICY SALSA CREAM:
1 **cup sour cream**
½ **cup tomatoes, minced**
1 **tablespoon red onion, minced**
1 **teaspoon jalapeno, seeded and minced**
1 **tablespoon fresh cilantro, minced**
¼ **cup fresh lime juice**
¼ **teaspoon kosher salt**
   lime wedge, for serving

Heat vegetable oil in a large pot over medium high heat, Season avocados with salt, to taste.
Working one at a time, dredge avocado slices in flour, dip into the egg, then dredge into the cornmeal pressing to coat.
Working in batches, add the avocado slices to the oil pot, 5 or 6 at a time, and fry until evenly golden brown and crispy, about 1-2 minutes on each side.
Transfer to a paper towel-lined plate. For the spicy salsa cream, add sour cream to a mixing bowl. Whisk together the remaining ingredients. Allow to sit for a few minutes to allow the flavors to come together.
To serve, arrange fried avocados on a plate with a spoonful of the spicy salsa cream, and a fresh lime wedge. *Serves 4*

#classic french onion soup

½ cup unsalted butter
4 onions, sliced
2 garlic cloves, chopped
2 bay leaves
2 fresh thyme sprigs
   kosher salt and freshly ground black pepper
1 cup white wine, about 1/2 bottle
3 heaping tablespoons all-purpose flour
1 quart beef broth
1 quart chicken broth
1 baguette, sliced
½ pound grated Gruyere

Melt the stick of butter in a large pot over medium heat. Add the onions, garlic, bay leaves, thyme, and salt and pepper and cook until the onions are very soft and caramelized, about 25 minutes.

Add the wine, bring to a boil, reduce the heat and simmer until the wine has evaporated and the onions are dry, about 5 minutes.

Discard the bay leaves and thyme sprigs. Dust the onions with the flour and give them a stir. Turn the heat down to medium low so the flour doesn't burn, and cook for 10 minutes.

Now add the two broths, bring the soup back to a simmer, and cook for 10 minutes. Season, to taste, with salt and pepper.

Ladle the soup into bowls, top each with 2 slices of bread and top with cheese. Put the bowls into the oven to toast the bread and melt the cheese. **Serves 4**

Chef Adrianne
Liked · July 23

Old Fashioned French Onion Soup on tonight at Chef Adrianne's!!!
www.chefadriannes.com — with

Like · Comment · Share

409 people **like this.**   Top Comments ▾

16 shares

Yummy.
Like · Reply · July 23 at 4:22pm via mobile

Omg ... I'm salivating
Like · Reply · 👍 1 · July 23 at 4:10pm via mobile

JOOOOYYYYYYY Joy
Like · Reply · 👍 1 · July 23 at 4:07pm

That place is great
Like · Reply · July 24 at 2:43pm

Yum!!!!!!!
Like · Reply · July 24 at 2:15pm

Yumii delicious 😊
Like · Reply · July 24 at 1:18pm via mobile

Rico
See Translation
Like · Reply · July 23 at 11:58pm via mobile

thats looks sooo goood!
Like · Reply · July 23 at 11:06pm via mobile

take me now!!!

I'm crazy about laying out cheese so that it melts and caramelizes perfectly around the soup bowl.

#whipped corn soup
wild mushroom ragu and mozzarella

8 ears corn, husked
2 tablespoons sugar
  salt and freshly ground black pepper
1 cup heavy cream
2 tablespoons bacon grease
1 tablespoons butter
¼ cup extra-virgin olive oil
1 large yellow onion, chopped
4 garlic cloves, minced
1 pound mixed mushrooms (cremini oyster, shii take) chopped , kosher salt and freshly ground black pepper, to taste
2 cups low sodium chicken broth
⅓ cup heavy cream
5 fresh basil leaves, chopped
¼ cup flat-leaf italian parsley, chopped
¼ cup grated parmesan
¼ cup marsala
1 cup mozzarella, shredded (for final step)

In a large bowl, cut the tip off cob. Cut the kernels from cob with a small paring knife.
Using the back of the blade, scrape against the cob to press out the milky liquid.
Whisk together sugar, and salt and pepper, to taste.
Combine with corn. Add the heavy cream and mix. In a large skillet over medium heat, cook bacon grease.
Add corn mixture and turn heat down to medium-low, stirring until it becomes creamy, about 20-25 minutes. Fold in butter. Then, cool slightly and place in a blender. Blend on medium-high speed for 30 seconds or until velvety consistency.
In a large skillet heat the oil. When almost smoking, add the onions and garlic over medium-low heat until the onions have wilted, about 10 minutes.
Add the mushrooms and season with salt and pepper. Raise heat to high and saute until mushrooms are tender and all the liquid has evaporated.
Remove pan from heat and pour in Marsala. Return pan to stove and allow wine to evaporate, about 4-5 minutes. Add chicken broth and simmer for 1/2 hour until the sauce has reduced by half. Add heavy cream and mix well. Take the

pan off the heat and add the fresh herbs and Parmesan and mix thoroughly.

TO SERVE:
Preheat broiler to high. Using an oven proof vessel, pour in whipped corn, top with mushroom ragú, then top with mozzarella. Place under broiler just long enough for the cheese to melt. I like to garnish it with chopped chives.
Serves 4

Chef Adrianne
Liked · October 3 ⦿

Our Whipped Corn + Truffled Cremini Mushroom Sugo + Mozzarella!!!
www.chefadriannes.com

Like · Comment · Share

👍 127 people like this.   Top Comments ▾

🗐 1 share

That looks amazing!!! Yum
Like · Reply · 👍 1 · October 4 at 10:27am via mobile

the deliciousness we are in store for on Saturday is going to be amazing.
Like · Reply · 👍 2 · October 3 at 9:25pm via mobile

Looks DELICIOUS Chef Adrianne!
Like · Reply · October 4 at 9:24am

hay mama que rico hummmmmmmmmmmm....
See Translation
Like · Reply · October 4 at 12:32am via mobile

Sounds amazing

Mint and Cilantro together = BOLD and REFRESHING

#grilled shrimp
mint cilantro chimichurri

2 **tablespoons garlic salt**
2 **tablespoons brown sugar**
2 **tablespoons paprika**
2 **tablespoons canola oil**
  juice of 2 lemons
  kosher salt and freshly ground black pepper
1 **pound large shrimp (16/20), shelled,**
  deveined, tails left on and patted dry
1 **cup tightly packed fresh cilantro leaves**
¼ **cup tightly packed fresh mint leaves**
¼ **cup tightly packed fresh parsley**
7 **scallions, chopped**
½ **jalapeno, seeded and minced**
  zest of 1 lime
2 **tablespoons honey**
2 **tablespoons canola oil**
  kosher salt and freshly ground black pepper
  sriracha, (optional)

In a medium mixing bowl, whisk together garlic salt, brown sugar, paprika, canola oil, lemon juice, salt and pepper. Add the shrimp and marinade for 20-30 minutes.

Meanwhile, combine all the ingredients for the mint-cilantro chimichurri in a food processor and blend until smooth. You might have to pause and scrape down the sides, and pulse a few times more.

Season with salt and pepper to taste and set aside.

For the shrimp, heat a grill pan or sauté pan to medium high heat. Add the shrimp and cook 1-2 minutes on each side or until opaque and begin to curl up. To serve, spoon the mint cilantro chimichurri on the dish, and then place the shrimp on top. If desired, make a line of Sriracha adjacent to the chimichurri for added heat.

Serves 4

#braised ham hock mac and cheese

5 tablespoons butter
5 tablespoons flour
3 ½ cups hot milk
   black pepper to taste
   sea salt to taste
½ cup white cheddar cheese
¼ cup parmesan cheese
2 teaspoons dijon mustard
1 shallot, sliced
7 garlic cloves, smashed
1 bay leaf
2 sprigs thyme
   grated nutmeg to taste
1 pound elbow macaroni, cooked al dente
1 ham hock (about 2 pounds), soaked in cold water
1 stick celery
1 small onion, peeled and cut in half
1 small leek, washed and cut in half
1 peeled carrot, split and halved
2 sprigs thyme
1 teaspoon black peppercorns
2 sprigs parsley
¼ cup clear honey

Bring the milk to a simmer with the herbs, spices (except salt and pepper), shallots and garlic. Turn off and leave for 20 minutes, covered with plastic wrap. Melt the butter in a pan on a low heat, then add the flour and cook for 5 minutes stirring regularly. While this is cooking, remove plastic from pot, remove bay leaf, and bring the milk back to simmer.

Add the milk all at once to the roux, pouring through a chinoise (or fine sieve) and whisking constantly, getting into the edges of the pan. Add the salt and pepper and bring to a slow simmer for 5 minutes, stirring all the time. Add the mustard and cheeses. Turn the heat off and pass the mixture through a fine sieve

Place the ham into a large pan of water and bring to a boil, then remove from the heat and refresh in cold running water for 5-10 minutes. Place back onto the heat and bring to a simmer. Skim off any scum, then add all of the ingredients. Bring this back up to a low simmer and cook for 4 hours, skimming as needed. Once the ham is cooked, carefully remove from stock. Remove skin and fat, and flake the meat into bite-size pieces.

- #tonight -

TO ASSEMBLE AND SERVE:
Preheat oven to 350 degrees. Over low heat in a large pot, mix hot pasta with the hot sauce and heat together, adding the braised, flaked ham hock. Divide into individual ramekins, topped with a sprinkle of grated cheddar cheese and Parmesan, and bake in the oven for about 5 minutes, or until bubbling.
Finish under the broiler for a brown, crispy crust. Serve immediately. **Serves 4**

 Chef Adrianne
Liked · Yesterday

Tonight at Chef Adrianne's it's return of the Mac with our outrageous Braised Ham Hock Four Cheese Truffle Mac!
www.chefadriannes.com

Like · Comment · Share

👍 and 124   Top Comments ▾
others **like this.**

 !!!!!!
So excited.... Can't wait!!!!!!!
Like · Reply · 16 hours ago

 Ummm
want to have a date night with me and share this??
Like · Reply · 👍 1 · 23 hours ago

 Oh my god.
Like · Reply · 👍 1 · Yesterday at 11:43am

Looks delicious

#brown sugar crusted salmon
sweet chili, garlic, potatoes

2 **(8 ounce) salmon fillets, skinned and boned**
1 **tablespoon brown sugar**
1 **tablespoon maximum flavor**
   essentials chef's dust
1 **cup canola oil, for frying plus more for coating**
¼ **cup mayonnaise**
¼ **cup sweet chili sauce**
1 **teaspoon garlic, minced**
1 **cup idaho potatoes, small dice**
1 **cup baby spinach**
   chipotle hot sauce, optional
   micro greens, garnish

In a deep sauce pot, heat oil to medium high heat. Meanwhile, season salmon fillets with brown sugar first then chef's dust.

Heat a large sauté pan to medium high with a tablespoon of canola oil. When it's hot, add salmon fillets seasoning side down first. Cook for 2-3 minutes. Do not move in order to made a great crust. Flip over and cook for another 2-3 minutes or until desired doneness is reached.

Add diced potatoes to hot oil and fry for 4-5 minutes. Remove from oil and drain on a paper towel lined plate. In the meantime, combine mayonnaise, sweet chili sauce, and garlic in small mixing bowl. When ready to plate add the mixture to a small sauté pan to warm up and add the potatoes. Add the spinach just too warm through and cook quickly.

Divide among two plates and top with the salmon fillets. Garnish with chipotle and micro greens. ***Serves 2***

- #tonight -

Elevating chicken wings to the upteenth level!

#honey miso marinated chicken lollipops
garlic truffle aioli

½ cup light soy sauce
½ cup miso paste
½ cup honey
1 tablespoon ginger, grated
1 tablespoon garlic, minced
1 teaspoon crushed red pepper flakes
1 dozen chicken lollipops (or drumettes that
   have been frenched)
1 cup mayonnaise
1 tablespoon garlic, minced
1 tablespoon white truffle oil
1 teaspoon lemon juice
   kosher salt and freshly ground black pepper

In a large mixing bowl, whisk together soy sauce, miso paste, honey, ginger, garlic, and red pepper flakes. Put the chicken lollipops in a resealable plastic bag and pour marinade over them. Refrigerate at least 4 hours or overnight. Preheat the oven to 425 degrees F.

Remove the chicken lollipops from marinade and pat dry. Place them on baking sheet and cook for 20-25 minutes, or until they have reached a golden caramelized color. Meanwhile, to make the aioli, combine all of the ingredients in a bowl, and whisk until well combined. Adjust salt and pepper to taste.

To serve, smear aioli on a dish and top with the lollipops. **Serves 4**

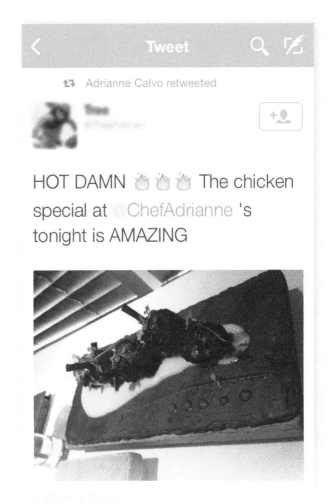

Adrianne Calvo retweeted

HOT DAMN 🔥🔥🔥 The chicken special at @ChefAdrianne 's tonight is AMAZING

#miso honey glazed snapper

2 tablespoons light or white miso
2 tablespoons honey
1 tablespoon garlic, minced
2 tablespoons white vinegar
4 (6-ounce) snapper fillets

Preheat the oven to 475 degrees F.
Whisk together the miso, honey, garlic, and vinegar in a small bowl. Lay the fish fillets in a 6 by 10-inch glass baking dish and brush with the glaze.
Put the dish in the oven on the middle rack and bake about 15 to 20 minutes. Remove from the oven and let rest in the dish for 5 minutes before serving. I serve this at the restaurant with our homemade mashed potatoes and sautéed spinach. ***Serves 4***

Chef Adrianne
Liked · May 28

Today's insane deliciousness! Miso Honey Glazed Florida Snapper + Soy Truffle Butter!
www.chefadriannes.com

Like · Comment · Share

and 501 others like this.   Top Comments ▾

31 shares

Sounds and looks amazing Chef! I bet my Wifey would love this!
Like · Reply · 1 · May 29 at 7:29pm

i wish i liked seafood, this sounds amazing
Like · Reply · June 3 at 11:46pm

Nela no seas golosa que engordas un besito de mery
See Translation
Like · Reply · May 30 at 8:51am

Oh no!! Butter....

I have two favorite ways of cooking as well as eating fish: French and Asian. Marinating any fish in a great miso mixture will result in an incredible end product. I also can't resist a simple lemon truffle butter... oooh lala :)

I always say I'm allergic to boring so I never wanted to create a standard duck dish. After tons of recipe testing, we realized that blueberries and duck create fireworks on the palette

#pan seared duck breast
blueberry sauce and fried blueberries

6 **large boneless duck breast fillets, skin on**
salt and freshly ground black pepper
2 **tablespoons canola oil**
¼ **cup balsamic vinegar**
1 **cup red wine**
1 **cup chicken or duck stock**
⅓ **cup brown sugar**
2 **cups wild blueberries, plus 1 cup for frying**
2 **tablespoons butter**

Season the duck breast with salt and pepper. Heat the oil in a large saute pan over medium-high heat. Brown the duck breast, skin side first, then flip over, reduce heat and cook other side, about 15 minutes.

Remove the duck breasts to a platter, reserving the juices in the pan. To make the sauce, add the balsamic vinegar and red wine to the pan and cook until reduced by half. Add the stock and reduce by half again, then add brown sugar, and blueberries and cook for 5 minutes.

Pour into a bowl and whisk in the butter to finish. Place the duck breast on each plate and drizzle the sauce around.

In a fryer or deep pan with hot oil, flash fry 1 cup of blueberries for 30 seconds or until skin starts to blister. Top the duck breasts with a couple of fried blueberries. ***Serves 6***

← PHOTO ⟳

chefadrianne ⏱ 6w

79 likes

chefadrianne Technique is just as important as creativity. Simple lessons like a very hot pan for searing, make the difference between a dish being good or a dish being great. This is our duck breast at Chef Adrianne's.
www.chefadriannes.com
#chefadriannes #maximumflavor #miami #bestof #restaurants #chef #technique
#musthave #drools
Technique is crucial. Sadly it is often overlooked
My wife and I are heading over tonight to celebrate our birthdays. We can't wait!

#grilled chicken
green onion ginger peanut relish

4 (8 ounce) Chicken breast, skinless , boneless
¼ cup brown sugar
¼ cup black pepper, freshly ground
¼ cup garlic salt
   canola oil
1 cup green onion, sliced
1 teaspoon ginger, grated
1 tablespoon red bell pepper, minced
1 teaspoon cilantro, minced
1 cup peanuts, roasted and chopped
1 tablespoon lime juice
1 teaspoon honey
   kosher salt and freshly ground black pepper

Heat a large skillet to medium high. Add canola oil. In a small mixing bowl combine brown sugar, garlic salt, and black pepper.

Season chicken breasts generously with spice blend. Place in hot skillet.

Cook 4-5 minutes on each side or until well done and juices run clear. In the meantime, in another mixing bowl, combine, green onions, ginger, bell pepper, cilantro, peanuts, lime, and honey.

Adjust seasoning with salt and pepper to taste. To serve, place a chicken breast on a plate and top with relish. Relish can be made up to 2 days in advance and stored in the refrigerator.

Serves 4

- #tonight -

Bold and exotic flavors can make chicken exciting
I always say Im allergic to boring and chicken can
sometimes get - "blah" Not with this recipe!

"It took over a year to develop and perfect this Porkbelly dish but after many flavor combinations and techniques, this is by far everyone's fave!"

using a high quality porkbelly
is super important in this
recipe. It makes all the difference
in texture in the finished product.

#asian braised berkshire pork belly
chinese hot honey mustard, sweet soy, pork rind crunch

1 pound berkshire pork belly, or high quality pork belly
1 cup light soy sauce
1 cup water
1 cup white vinegar
½ cup garlic, minced
1 cup granulated sugar
1 cup sweet chili
½ cup chinese hot mustard
½ cup honey
¼ cup water
½ cup sweet soy
1 cup pork rinds, store bought, ground

Preheat the oven to 350 degrees F.

In a large mixing bowl, whisk together soy sauce, water, vinegar, sugar, garlic, and sweet chili. Place pork belly in a baking dish and pour mixture over the top.

The pork belly should be covered on all sides with the liquid.

Cover with aluminum and bake for 2 hours or until fork tender. The pork belly should pull apart with a fork.

Meanwhile, in a medium mixing bowl whisk together hot mustard, honey, and water. Set aside.

To plate, spoon hot honey mustard and sweet soy sauce on plate. Place pork belly on top. Garnish with ground pork rinds and edible flowers.

Serves 4

Chef Adrianne
Liked · August 4

Tonight's slow cooked Neiman Ranch Pork Belly right out of the oven at Chef Adrianne's!!! www.chefadriannes.com — with

Like · Comment · Share

👍 389 people like this.   Top Comments ▾

🗐 3 shares

QUE RICO!!!! tengo pancito para el juguito!!!!Jaja.
See Translation
Like · Reply · August 4 at 9:56pm

Looks delicious. ..   ✕
Like · Reply · August 5 at 3:08pm via mobile

Jesus. I just gained 5 lbs looking at this picture
Like · Reply · August 4 at 9:49pm

#double-cut berkshire pork chop
maple glazed shallot pan sauce

2 **(24 ounce) pork chop, double cut and trimmed**
1 **teaspoon brown sugar**
½ **teaspoon garlic salt**
½ **teaspoon black pepper**
½ **teaspoon paprika**
¼ **cup butter**
½ **cup**
½ **cup maple syrup, (high quality)**
½ **whole shallots, sliced in quarters**
   kosher salt and freshly ground black pepper

Preheat the oven to 450 degrees F.
Preheat a large skillet to medium high heat. Add the butter and allow to melt slowly.
Skim off excess fat solids from the melted butter.
Meanwhile, season pork chops with brown sugar, garlic salt, paprika, and black pepper. Place seasoned pork chops in the skillet and sear for 4-5 minutes to create a nice crust.
Once the pork chops are seared, remove them from the skillet and place on a baking sheet. Do not discard the pan with the butter, you will use it for the sauce.
Place pork chops in preheated oven and roast for 12-15 minutes or until desired doneness.
Using the pan with the butter that was used to sear the pork chops, add the shallots.
Cook shallots for 3-5 minutes or until they start to caramelize. Stir in maple syrup and cook for an additional 3-5 minutes.

Adjust pan sauce with salt and pepper according to your liking. When ready to serve, spoon shallot pan sauce over pork chop and enjoy. ***Serves 2***

" Pan sauces are great and they are quick. They can dress up any protein and make them look fancy in a short amount of time. A great pan sauce packs a punch – of flavor! For this pan sauce, we could throw in a couple more ingredients for fun, like peaches or apricots. "

Chef Adrianne Calvo
August 19

Our Vermont Maple Glazed Berkshire Pork Chop + Truffle Au Jus!
www.chefadriannes.com

Like · Comment · Share   2 Shares

43 people like this.

   Esa carne es un sueño en el paraíso
See Translation

- #tonight -

Simply put: OUT OF CONTROL!

For this prime beef tartare, I usually use Black Angus but for a special occasion, I like to use Wagyu beef.

#prime beef tartare

12 ounce prime beef tenderloin or sirloin
    assorted micro greens
    worcestershire sauce
    hot pepper sauce
1 garlic clove, minced
    kosher salt
    freshly cracked black pepper
2 tablespoon drained capers
2 tablespoon dijon mustard
⅓ cup minced red onion
⅓ cup finely chopped parsley
1 egg
4 slices of white bread, crusts removed, brushed
    with olive oil and lightly toasted extra virgin
    olive oil

Place the beef on a cutting board and finely chop with garlic then, season to taste with Worcestershire sauce, hot pepper sauce, salt and black pepper.

Pat down tartare thinly and plate on a serving dish. On top of the beef, arrange the capers, Dijon mustard, red onion, parsley, and micro greens.

Carefully break the egg, reserving the yolk. Place the yolk in the center of the tartare. Serve the steak tartare with toast points. **Serves 2**

Chef Adrianne
Liked · August 7

Tonight's Prime Beef Tartare + French Trimmings + Parmesan Crisp + Truffled Quail Egg!
www.chefadriannes.com

Like · Comment · Share

👍 126 people like this.   Top Comments ▾

4 shares

Divino, que presentacion
See Translation
Like · Reply · August 8 at 7:47am via mobile

Taking notes
Like · Reply · August 8 at 12:20am via mobile

Looks great and I'm sure tastes better!!!
Like · Reply · August 7 at 11:49pm

Yummmmm!!

" Life is full of surprises. When we opened
Chef Adrianne's I said I wald <u>never</u>
make steaks. After a ton of requests,
I gave in. I gave in with one
condition, to try to make the best
steak in town. Today, people come
from everywhere for our steaks.
Funny Story I guess. "

#chef adrianne's filet mignon
sauce au poivre

4 tenderloin steaks, 12-16 ounces each
   kosher salt and freshly ground black
   peppercorns
1 tablespoon unsalted butter

SAUCE AU POIVRE:
1 tablespoon coarsely ground black pepper
1 tablespoon vegetable oil
2 tablespoons chopped shallots
1 tablespoon drained, rinsed, and crushed
   whole peppercorns
½ cup brandy
1 tablespoon dijon mustard
2 cups veal reduction

VEAL REDUCTION:
4 pounds veal bones with some meat
   attached, sawed into 2-inch pieces
2 tablespoons olive oil
2 cups coarsely chopped yellow onions
1 cup coarsely chopped carrots
1 cup coarsely chopped celery
5 garlic cloves, peeled and smashed
¼ cup tomato paste
6 quarts water
2 bay leaves
1 teaspoon dried thyme
1 teaspoon kosher salt
1 teaspoon whole black peppercorns
2 cups dry red wine

Place the black pepper in a dry small saucepan and toast over medium-high heat until fragrant, 1 to 2 minutes. Add the oil and stir to combine. Add the shallots and peppercorns, and cook, stirring, for 30 seconds. Remove the pan from the heat, add the brandy, return to the heat to flambe, then simmer until reduced by three-quarters. Add the mustard and stir, then add the veal reduction and bring to a boil. Reduce the heat to medium-low and simmer until reduced by half, about 15 minutes.

VEAL REDUCTION:
Preheat the oven to 375 degrees F.
Place the bones in a large roasting pan and toss with the oil. Roast, turning occasionally, until golden brown, about 1 hour. Remove from the oven and spread the onions, carrots, celery, and garlic over the bones.
Smear the tomato paste over the vegetables and return the pan to the oven.
Roast for another 45 minutes. Remove from the oven and pour off the fat from the pan. Transfer the bones and vegetables to a large stockpot.
Add the water, bay leaves, thyme, salt, and peppercorns to the stockpot and bring to a boil. Meanwhile, place the roasting pan over 2 burners on medium-high heat.

Add the wine and stir with a heavy wooden spoon to deglaze any browned bits clinging to the bottom of the pan. Add the contents to the stockpot. When the liquid returns to a boil, reduce the heat to low and simmer, uncovered, for 8 hours, skimming occasionally to remove any foam that rises to the surface.

Ladle through a fine-mesh strainer into a large clean pot. Bring to a boil, reduce to a simmer, and cook, uncovered, until reduced to 6 cups in volume, about 1-2 hours. Let cool, then cover and refrigerate overnight.

Remove any congealed fat from the surface of the stock.

Remove the steaks from the refrigerator for at least 30 minutes and up to 1 hour prior to cooking.

Sprinkle all sides with salt and pepper. In a medium skillet over medium heat, melt the butter. As soon as the butter begins to turn golden and smoke, gently place the steaks in the pan.

For medium-rare, cook for 4 minutes on each side. For additional doneness, add 1-2 minutes per side. Allow to rest 10 minutes before serving. **Serves 4**

 Chef Adrianne
Liked · July 6

There are steaks... And then there's Our Steaks!
www.chefadriannes.com

Like · Comment · Share

 157 people like this.   Top Comments ▾

Still the best filet mignon ive ever had 😊
Like · Reply · 👍 1 · July 6 at 9:51am via mobile

She is one of th best chef that I know
Like · Reply · July 6 at 2:53pm

The hubby is drooling looking at this steak!! Yum!!
Like · Reply · July 6 at 1:55pm via mobile

Woooowww luce deliiicioooosooo
See Translation
Like · Reply · July 6 at 9:55am via mobile

Mmmmm, yummy,
Like · Reply · July 6 at 9:53am via mobile

#fried doughnuts
sea salt and condensed milk

3 cups all-purpose flour
1 cup of water
1 teaspoon baking powder
¼ teaspoon baking soda
1 teaspoon sugar
1 tablespoon vegetable oil
½ cup condensed milk
1 teaspoon sea salt for sprinkling
1 tablespoon powdered sugar

Mix baking soda, baking powder, salt and sugar. Add water and stir well. Add this mixture to the all-purpose flour and stir for a few seconds. Add vegetable oil and mix until well combined.

Cover and leave it for 4 hours at room temperature.

Heat oil in a frying pan. Dust work surface with flour. Roll the dough into a sausage shape. Cut into 1" pieces and then form a ball.

Carefully drop doughnuts 2 at a time into hot oil and fry it until they rise to the surface and are golden.

Toss the doughnuts in powdered sugar and sprinkle them with sea salt. Serve with condensed milk. ***Serves 8***

Chef Adrianne Calvo
19 hours ago via mobile

Tonight's Doughnuts!!!
www.chefadriannes.com

🏷 Tag Photo   📍 Add Location   ✏ Edit

Like · Comment · Unfollow Post · Share · Edit

👍 _____ and 9 others like this.

_____ Condensed milk...yum
18 hours ago · Unlike · 👍 1

_____ OMG...that looks soooo good!!!!!

When I think about comfort food I think of these donuts

This is a rendition of
our goat cheese appetizer
in dessert form and its
just as great!

#goat cheese cheesecake
raspberry sorbet and gold leaf

2 **cups graham cracker crumbs**

6 **tablespoons melted butter, plus extra butter for pan**

¼ **cup sugar**

pinch salt

2 **(8 ounce) package of cream cheese, at room temperature**

1 **(12 ounce) log goat cheese**

12 **ounces sour cream**

4 **eggs**

1 **cup sugar**

1 **tablespoon vanilla extract**

2 **cups fresh raspberries**

powdered sugar

raspberry sorbet

Preheat the oven to 350 degrees F.

Stir all of the ingredients together in a large bowl. Butter a 9-inch spring form pan. Press the crumb mixture onto the bottom and about halfway up the sides of the pan.

Beat the cream and goat cheese in the bowl of an electric mixer with the paddle attachment until light and fluffy. Add the sour cream and beat. Add the eggs, 1 at a time, beating after each egg is added, until thoroughly combined. Beat in the sugar and vanilla.

Pour the filling into the prepared crust. Put on a baking sheet in the preheated oven and bake for 55 to 60 minutes. Rotate the baking sheet halfway through the cooking process.

Top with fresh raspberries and dust powdered sugar over the top. I like to serve it with raspberry sorbet as well. *Serves 8*

Chef Adrianne
Liked · October 3

Tonight's French Goat Cheese Cheese Cake + Raspberry Marmalade + Raspberry Sorbet + White Chocolate Crunch!
www.chefadriannes.com

Like · Comment · Share

👍 64 people like this.   Top Comments ▾

Sounds and looks amazing!!
Like · Reply · 👍 1 · October 3 at 11:09pm via mobile

Food pornography, Chef Adrianne!!! Which is why we love it!!
Like · Reply · October 4 at 7:14pm

#peanut butter pie

1 ½ cups heavy whipping cream
¼ cup sugar
8 ounces cream cheese
1 cup creamy peanut butter
1 cup confectioners' sugar
1 graham cracker crust, premade

Whip cream with 1/4 cup sugar.
Mix all other ingredients until smooth and fold in whipped cream until well blended. Pour mixture into a graham cracker crust and chill for several hours before serving. Top with whipped cream, chocolate ganache, and salted pretzels.
Serves 8

Chef Adrianne
Liked · February 19

Tonight's Peanut Butter Cup Pie!!! It was Ridiculous!!!
www.chefadriannes.com

Unlike · Comment · Share

👍 You and 404 others like this.   Top Comments ▾

🗐 18 shares

Chef Adrianne is creative, inventive and just incredibly talented! BTW, her pomegranate sangria is also amazing!
Like · Reply · 👍 1 · February 20 at 9:38am

That really looks tasty!
Like · Reply · 👍 1 · February 20 at 8:34am

lolol I'm drooling !!!
Like · Reply · February 20 at 7:13pm

Weakness..
Like · Reply · February 20 at 11:13am

Ohh sweet Jesus I need a whole pan to myself asap
Like · Reply · February 20 at 10:58am

i want
Like · Reply · February 20 at 12:42am

I'm coming down to check you out Chef

Chocolate Peanut Butter Cups are my favorite chocate candy in the whole wide world so this is my way of making it an outrageous dessert. The cool part, is how easy it is to make!

Butterscotch and caramel. Very similar
But when put together, you can taste
their delicious differences.

#butterscotch budino
salted caramel gelato, salted caramel crisp

BUDINO:

3 cups heavy whipping cream
1 ½ cups whole milk
1 large egg
3 large egg yolks
¼ cup cornstarch
1 cup plus 2 tablespoons dark brown sugar
½ cup water
1 ½ teaspoons kosher salt
5 tablespoons unsalted butter
1 tablespoon dark rum
½ tablespoon scotch whiskey
1 teaspoon vanilla extract

SALTED CARAMEL:

1 cup whole milk
4 large egg yolks
¾ cup sugar
2 cups heavy cream
1 ¼ cups sugar
¾ cup heavy cream
2 teaspoons flaky sea salt, such as maldon
2 tablespoons vanilla extract

SALTED CARAMEL CRISP:

1 cup sugar
½ teaspoon flaky sea salt

BUDINO:

Mix cream and milk in large bowl. Whisk egg yolks, and cornstarch in medium bowl. Stir sugar, 1/2 cup water, and salt in heavy large pot over medium-low heat until sugar dissolves. Increase heat to medium-high and boil without stirring until mixture turns thick.

When mixture reached a deep tan color, begin stirring occasionally swirling pot and brushing down sides with wet pastry brush, about 7 minutes. Immediately whisk in cream mixture. Stir to dissolve caramel bits. Bring mixture to boil, watching closely to prevent mixture from pouring out, then reduce heat to medium.

Gradually whisk half of hot caramel mixture into egg mixture. Return mixture to pot, whisking to blend. Whisk over medium heat until custard slightly boils and is thickened, about 2-3 minutes. Remove from heat. Add butter, rum, scotch, and vanilla extract; stir until melted and smooth. Strain.

GELATO BASE:

Heat the milk in a sauce pan over medium-low heat. Prepare an ice bath by setting a bowl over a larger bowl halfway filled with ice water.

Place a strainer over the smaller bowl and set aside.

In a separate bowl, whisk together the egg

yolks and sugar until pale yellow in color and the sugar has dissolved.

Gradually pour the warmed milk into the yolk mixture, whisking vigorously. Pour the mixture back into the same saucepan you used to warm the milk.

Cook for 4- 5 minutes, stirring constantly, until the custard thickens and coats the back of a wooden spoon.

Strain the custard into the top bowl of the ice bath to stop the cooking process. Add the heavy cream and stir over the ice bath until cool. Cover the bowl with plastic wrap and chill thoroughly.

SALTED CARAMEL:

Heat the sugar in a dry heavy-bottomed sauce pan over medium heat, stirring to heat the sugar evenly, until it starts to melt. Continue cooking until it is a dark amber color.

Carefully add the heavy cream and cook, stirring until all the caramel has dissolved. Transfer to a heat-proof bowl and stir in the sea salt. Set the caramel mixture over a bowl filled with ice water and stir until chilled to room temperature.

Combine the caramel mixture with the gelato base and add the vanilla. Pour into a gelato maker or ice cream machine and follow manufacturer's instructions for churning and freezing.

SALTED CARAMEL CRISP:

In a heavy-bottomed sauce pan, melt 1 cup of sugar over medium high heat. Stir and cook until the sugar becomes an amber color. Pour onto wax paper or a nonstick work surface and immediately sprinkle with flaky sea salt. Allow to harden at room temperature.

To assemble, spoon a serving of budino into a serving dish. Top with salted caramel gelato and caramel crisp. ***Serves 8***

#classic chocolate mousse
belgian chocolate ganache

2 **cups heavy cream, very cold**
4 **large egg yolks**
½ **cup sugar**
1 **teaspoon vanilla**
1 **cup fine-quality semi -sweet chocolate, chopped**
  pinch of kosher salt
1 **cup belgian semi-sweet chocolate, chopped**
½ **cup heavy cream**
1 **teaspoon instant coffee**

BELGIAN CHOCOLATE GANACHE:
Cook the chocolate chips, heavy cream, and instant coffee in the top of a double boiler over simmering water until melted and smooth.
Beat remaining 1 ¼ cups cream in a bowl with an electric mixer until it forms stiff peaks. Whisk one fourth of cream into chocolate custard to lighten, then, fold in remaining cream.
Refrigerate mousse covered, at least 6 hours before serving. Top with Belgian chocolate ganache.
Heat 3/4 cup cream in a heavy saucepan until hot. Whisk together yolks, sugar, and a pinch of salt in a mixing bowl until combined well, then add hot cream in a slow stream, whisking until combined.
Transfer mixture to saucepan and cook over moderately low heat, stirring constantly for 3-4 minutes. Pour custard through a fine-mesh sieve into a bowl and stir in vanilla.

Melt chocolate in a double boiler, stirring frequently. Whisk custard into chocolate until smooth, then cool. **Serves 4**

chefadrianne   🕐 1w

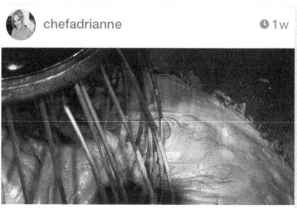

💜 106 likes

chefadrianne The making of our Mont Saint Michel style Chocolate Mousse!!! Tonight's dessert special at Chef Adrianne's!!! www.chefadriannes.com @eggandthecity #chefadriannes #maximumflavor #miami #restaurants #miamispice #maximumflavorsocial #dessert #chocolate #french

😍😍😍😍😍

😳

Decadence
Personified

For Sorbets, it makes
such an impact making
them from scratch.
The fresh fruit comes
foward in a vibrant
burst of flavor!

#raspberry sorbet

2 **cups sugar**
2 **cups water**
2 **quarts raspberries, hulled and sliced**
¼ **cup fresh lemon juice**
½ **cup light corn syrup**

Bring the sugar and 2 cups water to a boil in a medium saucepan over medium-high heat. Reduce the heat and allow the mixture to simmer, 3 minutes. Set aside to cool.

Place the raspberries and lemon juice in a food processor and puree. Press the raspberry puree through a strainer to remove the seeds. When the sugar syrup has cooled completely, combine with the raspberry puree. Add the corn syrup mix well.

Pour the mixture into an ice cream maker and freeze according to manufacturer's instructions.
Serves 4

#s'mores haute hot chocolate

1 cup milk, whole
1 cup heavy cream
¼ cup cocoa powder
2 tablespoons dark chocolate shavings
½ cup sugar
1 teaspoon instant coffee
¼ teaspoon vanilla extract
1 pinch salt
   graham cracker, crushed
½ cup mini marshmallows

Preheat oven to low broil and move oven rack to the second from the top. Place baking sheet on rack. Heat milk and heavy cream in a saucepan, over medium heat until it simmers – about 5 minutes. Be careful not to scald. Add cocoa powder, chocolate shavings, sugar, instant coffee, vanilla, and salt.

Whisk until thoroughly combined. Pour hot chocolate into two mugs and top with 1/4 cup marshmallows each.

Carefully set mugs on the baking sheet in the oven and broil marshmallows until browned, watching carefully. (They can burn in a few seconds). Remove from the oven with a towel and allow to cool for a few minutes. Top with crushed graham cracker crumbs and extra chocolate shavings. **Serves 2**

" What gives this hot chocolate an elegant flavor is the instant coffee. It brings forward the flavor of the chocolate. You'd be surprised it tastes nothing like coffee."

THE GREATEST INGREDIENT A CHEF CAN EVER USE IS LOVE

One of the popular sentiments out there about social media is that it has a real addictive quality, and we all probably know at least a couple of people who do nothing to disprove that theory! While I don't count myself as a total junkie (only because I'm usually in a kitchen!), I obviously give major props to this whole medium as a huge catalyst in my career and in helping me connect with a global network of guests, friends and family, being able to share an inside look at my passion with them in an extremely personal way. For example, just a few short years ago, the idea of a chef being able to take their guests through the evolutionary experience of creating a dish, starting from picking ingredients at a local farm to putting the final touches on the finished product, was unheard of! These days, thanks to social media, I'm able to take my friends and followers through that amazing process first-hand!

And yes, speaking of "addictive", I confess that I've most definitely felt a high for my craft as a direct result of interactions and feedback I've received on places like Facebook, Instagram, and Twitter. Having guests and followers show appreciation for my cooking has truly motivated me on a level that I didn't know existed, and continues to push me to keep creating something even better than the previous dish every single day. Of course, had you told me I'd feel anything remotely like this just 5 short years ago, I would have seen you as all sorts of crazy!

As I mentioned in the previous chapter, it took me some time to really even begin to warm up to the notion of posting anything that offered an inside look at what was happening on any given day at Chef Adrianne's. In fact, you could say I was just a tiny bit out of the loop at first; when my PR reps initially attempted to get me to try out Facebook, I rejected the idea by very adamantly explaining that I "don't do all that MySpace stuff". Obviously I was real hip to what was happening. Not!!

Mind you, I'd had a couple of websites dedicated to my cooking and product line by this stage, but I saw those as very low maintenance forms of long-term, ongoing promotion that had nothing "real-time" about them whatsoever. When it came to actually digitally updating people on any kind of regular basis or interacting with them in a public way, I really was a total newbie. In spite of my resistance, my reps persevered and got me to break the ice by opening up my Facebook account in 2009. Since I was still a bit of a skeptic, they also helped out with postings in those early days. It was during this time when we first had a couple of "coming out parties" on my page for some of our specials at the restaurant. My personal turning point came when I was alerted to the fact that I had a few positive comments underneath those pics; almost instantly, I started to see the whole social media thing in a whole new light. Talk about your true "OMG" moments!

From that point forward, you could say the floodgates swung open! Posting, updating, and interacting on Facebook became a "must" for me and started to play an essential role in my daily routine. Then, when Instagram came along a couple of years later, a whole new dimension was added to my personal social media universe. A picture most definitely says it all, and the culinary arts and a visual medium like Instagram are truly a perfect marriage. Immediate, easy, and quick are the perfect words to sum up the whole process of capturing a shot of our latest Maximum Flavor delicacy and posting it to Instagram, and it's become my go-to network where I first announce and display our specials each day.

Before I knew it, all of this very public and pretty much instant feedback I began to receive through social media got me "addicted" to pushing my limits as a chef. The

"social media got me addicted"

whole concept of people thriving off of positive reinforcement is totally true, and as a professional chef, this really manifests itself in my life every day. It is a beautiful challenge to try to top yourself each time you are doing something you completely love to do anyhow, and at the same time getting a crystal clear picture of how well you might be doing it from those whose opinion truly matters- your guests!

With this window they offer to what my fans and followers want and like, my social networks really have played a ginormous part in making the job of trying to offer my guests a memorable experience much easier. Back in the day for example, when my mom was whipping up those incredible dinners I told you about earlier, she had to wait until we took those first bites to really get a sense of how on point she'd been with her skills that day. Meanwhile, I have the luxury of instant feedback and gratification, which I have to admit, is very easy to get used to! The fact that my guests often feel the need to digitally share their satisfaction over their Maximum Flavor experience- usually before they even push back from the table!- is a really unique form of motivation for me to keep striving to create and innovate in the kitchen. The greatest ingredient a chef can ever use is love; when that love is not only shared but reciprocated, it makes me love what I do that much more!

The icing on the cake (to use a fitting play on words!) is when all of the positive comments and hype directly equal more guests actually coming through my door. After years of consistent posting and interaction, I can truly say that it all translates into raising the profile of the restaurant and the Maximum Flavor brand, and naturally, attracting more people to Chef Adrianne's. Social media plus a great restaurant ethic that supports delicious food and terrific service in a comfortable atmosphere really does make for a winning formula.

Beyond just serving as a benefit to the bottom line however, feeling truly connected to my guests and their experience at my restaurant has also given me a joy I never could have imagined I'd have. Perhaps the perfect ex-

ample that really crystallizes what the power of that connection can produce is the story of a family from India that had followed me on Facebook for years and then came down to Miami for a vacation. I'm proud to say that eating at Chef Adrianne's was on their itinerary. After they finished dinner the night they stopped in, they made it a point to say that it was all of my postings on Facebook which made their mouths water day after day that practically compelled them to come by and satisfy their cravings!

All in all, social media has truly allowed me to tap into the positive energy that good food seems to bring out in all of us and really create the anticipation that comes from looking at a vivid picture of a delicious dish. And make no mistake, foodies are a passionate bunch- in addition to many awesome compliments from online friends and followers I've been lucky to receive, I'm also flattered to say that I've even scored a marriage proposal or two from posting some of our specials. Now that's what I call being "Connected"!

This moment right there, I can't put into words how happy it makes me to create some thing right Infront of our guests

#connected
recipe index

#grilled chicken, mango, cucumber and feta salad

1 **tablespoon extra virgin olive oil**
1 **tablespoon lemon juice, freshly squeezed**
1 **tablespoon honey**
   kosher salt and black pepper, to taste
½ **cup mango, thinly sliced**
½ **cup cucumber, rough chopped**
¼ **cup red onion, thinly sliced**
½ **cup feta cheese, crumbled**
2 **cups organic baby spinach, rinsed**
2 **boneless, skinless chicken breasts, fully cooked**
   and sliced

In a mixing bowl, whisk together olive oil, lemon juice, and honey to make the dressing. Season with salt and pepper to taste.

Add the rest of the ingredients into the bowl, using a pair of salad tongs, toss lightly just to coat all the ingredients evenly.

Tip: This is a great way to use left -over chicken. Chicken can also be exchanged for beef or shrimp. Dressing can be made up to 3-5 days ahead and stored in the refrigerator. *Serves 2*

"I developed this easy and delicious recipe after asking all my Facebook friends, "What was their favorite ingredient in a summer salad?" Mango was the winner! Mango, chicken, and feta are magical!."

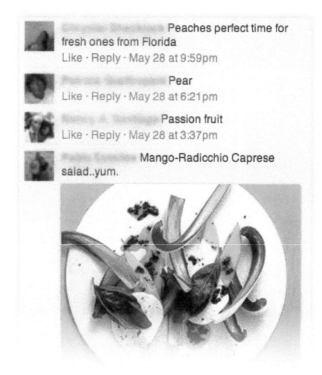

Peaches perfect time for fresh ones from Florida
Like · Reply · May 28 at 9:59pm

Pear
Like · Reply · May 28 at 6:21pm

Passion fruit
Like · Reply · May 28 at 3:37pm

Mango-Radicchio Caprese salad..yum.

Mango and feta surprisingly go
so well together. Sharp saltiness
of the feta holds a nice
contrast to rich and sweet mango

This was actually the first recipe written and first photo taken for this book :)

#plantain soup

2 tablespoons extra -virgin olive oil
1 small yellow onion, finely chopped
1 carrot, peeled and finely chopped
1 celery rib, strings removed and finely chopped
8 garlic cloves, finely chopped
4 ½ cups chicken broth, homemade or canned
   low-sodium broth, plus more if needed
2 green plantains, peeled and thinly sliced
1 cup fresh cilantro leaves, finely chopped
2 bay leaves
½ teaspoon ground cumin
   kosher salt and fresh ground black pepper
½ cup chorizo, crumbled and fried

Heat the olive oil in a saucepan over medium-high heat for 1-2 minutes.

Add the onions, carrots, celery, and garlic and cook until the onions are soft and browned, 8-10 minutes, stirring often with a wooden spoon.

Add the chicken stock, plantains, cilantro, bay leaves and cumin, and bring to a boil, reduce the heat to the lowest setting and cook at a bare simmer, uncovered, until the plantains are very tender, 45 minutes.

Transfer half of the soup to a blender and puree until smooth. When blending hot liquids, fill the blender less than halfway full, place the lid and pulse the liquid at first to release some heat. Repeat until all the soup is pureed. If the soup is too thick for your taste add more chicken stock. Season with salt and pepper, top with crispy chorizo and serve. *Serves 4*

#candied jalapeno new zealand lamb chops

12 baby lamb chops
 olive oil
 salt and freshly ground pepper
4 pounds fresh jalapeno peppers, sliced
2 pounds onions, diced
 cup vinegar
 cup water
6-8 cups sugar
2 tablespoons mustard seeds
1 teaspoon turmeric
2 teaspoons celery seeds (optional)
1 fresh garlic cloves (1 per jar)
1 teaspoon ginger

LAMB CHOPS:
Preheat grill to high. Brush chops on both sides with olive oil and season with salt and pepper. Grill for 2 to 3 minutes on both sides for medium-rare doneness. Remove from grill and top with candied jalapenos. Garnish with green onions.

CANDIED JALAPENOS:
Slice Jalapenos into thin slices and dice onions (I would suggest a pair of rubber gloves for handling jalapenos, personal experience, do not touch your face!). Place in pan with water and vinegar, bring to a boil, reduce heat & simmer about 2 min. (do not breath fumes).
Pour off most of the water vinegar mixture, add the sugar and spices. Bring to soft candy temperature to completely dissolve sugar about another 10 minute Place boiling mixture into jars, leaving 1/4 inch head space. Adjust caps.
Serves 4

102

In my opinion New Zealand has the best lamb on the planet. Their lamb is raised with the highest standards I've ever known. It reflects in the flavor.

I'm secretly addicted to Sriracha

#sliced tuna
white truffle soy garlic aioli

8 **ounce saku block, or sushi grade**
  tuna, sliced ¼ inch thick
2 **ounce lotus root, sliced paper thin**
1 **cucumber, peeled lengthwise to make ribbons**
¼ **cup mayonnaise**
1 **teaspoon garlic, minced**
1 **tablespoon light soy sauce**
½ **teaspoon white truffle oil**
1 **teaspoon lemon juice**
1 **teaspoon honey**
  canola oil for frying
  sriracha, optional

In a small pot heat oil on medium high to quickly fry sliced lotus root chips just until crispy. About 1 minute. Set aside on a paper towel to drain. In a mixing bowl, using a whisk combine mayonnaise, garlic, soy, lemon, truffle, and honey. To assemble dish, spoon some of the sauce on a dish, then lay sliced tuna on top. Garnish with cucumber ribbons and lotus root chips. *Serves 2*

I think this dish is an amazing way to start a spectacular meal, but I 'd prefer it with a little heat so I add sriracha on the side. That's why I put optional on this recipe, but in my opinion, its a must! If you can't find sriracha, any asian chili sauce will work

#roasted asparagus
crisp prosciutto, balsamic reduction

16 asparagus spears, preferably organic
16 thin prosciutto slices
   extra virgin olive oil
   kosher salt and freshly cracked black pepper
¼ cup parmesan shavings
½ cup balsamic vinegar
1 tablespoon sugar

Preheat the oven to 400 degrees F.

On a clean work surface, roll one slice of prosciutto around one asparagus spear.

Repeat this step for all 16 spears. Drizzle olive oil on a baking sheet and place the wrapped asparagus on it.

Bake for 10-12 minutes or until prosciutto begins to crisp and asparagus starts to brown at the tips. Meanwhile, in a small sauce pan over medium heat, whisk together balsamic vinegar sugar.

Simmer for a few minutes or until reduced by half. To serve, drizzle balsamic reduction on the plate. Place asparagus in center of plate.

Season with salt and pepper to taste, then top with parmesan shavings. *Serves: 4*

- #connected -

This is an elegant appetizer that isn't too complicated. It goes perfectly with an oaky and buttery Chardonnay

#crispy gouda
raspberry sauce

4 (1-inch-thick) slices of gouda cheese
   salt to taste
½ cup all-purpose flour
1 large beaten egg
2/3 cup panko bread crumbs
   oil or shortening for frying
2 cups raspberries
1 tablespoon sugar
1 teaspoon lemon juice

Sprinkle cheese with salt. Dredge slices in flour, then in beaten egg, and finally in panko bread crumbs, making sure the cheese slices are completely covered. Fry quickly in hot oil or shortening until golden brown. Serve immediately.

RASPBERRY PRESERVES:
Combine all ingredients in a saucepan and cook until broken down about 15 minutes. Can be made up to 3 days ahead and stored in refrigerator.

For this recipe, you can use normal bread crumbs to bread the gouda, however, I like panko because its crispier. It elevates the fried cheese experience.

For the raspberry sauce, you can strain it through a chinois after cooking it if you don't like the seeds. I like the seeds. *Serves 2*

#lobster crudo fra diavolo

½ **pound cold water lobster tail, lightly poached, chilled**
½ **lemon, juiced**
2 **garlic cloves, minced**
1 **tablespoon capers**
2 **tablespoon italian parsley, minced**
1 **jalapeno or serrano chile, sliced into paper thin rings**
  sprinkles of hawaiian black lava salt or
  coarse sea salt
2 **turns fresh black pepper**
4 **teaspoons extra-virgin cold-pressed olive oil**

Slice lobster tails ¼ inch thick. In a mixing bowl, toss lobster slices with lemon, garlic, capers, parsley, chiles, salt, pepper, and olive oil. Let sit in refrigerator for at least 20 minutes. To serve, arrange like a log on a plate. Garnish with extra chile greens and lemon wedges. **Serves 4**

This is an exciting alternative to ceviche. Plus, it works marvelously with a glass of chilled Sauvignon Blanc!

Baking or crispy-ing up Italian deli meats brings foward their flavor and intensifies it.

#hot capicola rolls

¼ pounds italian hot capicola, thinly sliced
1 log aluette sundried tomaotes and garlic
1 slice toasted garlic bread or a handful of garlic croutons, crushed
¼ cup balsamic glaze, (bottled or balsamic vinegar reduced by half)

Preheat oven to 400 degrees Farenheit.

On a clean work surface, lay out the capicola and place a heaping spoonful of Aluette cheese on one end. Roll up to make a tight log.

Repeat for the remaining cheese and capicola. Place on a baking sheet and cook in oven for 3-5 minutes just to heat through an melt cheese slightly.

Top with crushed garlic bread or garlic croutons. Drizzle with a qood quality balsamic glaze Enjoy! *Serves 4*

PHOTO

chefadrianne

79 likes

chefadrianne This was one of the four dishes that won national first place for Allouette™ Cheese Master Chef Competition! Baked Hot Capicola with whipped Allouette™ Sundried Tomato and Garlic Cheese + Parmesan Bread Crumbs! #chefadriannes #maximumflavor #bestof #miami #restaurants #chef

Deberiamos d ir por el cumple d cari

Nice!

Omg....I'm hungry. Amazing.

, this is the restaurant I was telling you about

♥ Like   ● Comment   •••

#butter poached maine lobster burrata

2 maine lobsters, each about 1 ½ pounds butter,
    enough for poaching (about 5 pounds)
1 ½ pounds heirloom tomatoes, preferably a mix
    of sizes and colors, sliced thinly
¼ cup fresh lemon juice
    kosher salt and freshly ground black pepper
1 teaspoon fresh lemon juice
1 teaspoon white truffle oil
    pinch of crushed red pepper
8 ounces burrata cheese
¼ cup garlic croutons, crushed
¼ cup pesto
    flaked sea salt

 Chef Adrianne Calvo
July 17

Tonight's Maine Lobster Burrata + Preserved Lemon
Vinaigrette + Crushed Garlic Bread + Truffle Sea Salt!
www.chefadriannes.com

Like · Comment · Share · Sponsored

👍 32 people like this.

I wish I didn't have to work..
July 18 at 6:39am · Like

oh wow
July 18 at 11:15am · Like

Bring a large pot of butter to a gentle simmer. Add the lobsters and cook uncovered for about 8 minutes. Check for doneness by twisting a tail off; the meat should be opaque throughout. If it's still translucent, continue cooking for another 1 to 2 minutes. Drain and let cool.

Remove the meat from the tails and claws and slice it into 1-inch pieces. Meanwhile, in a medium bowl, add lemon juice, salt and pepper, truffle oil, and crushed red pepper. Add the lobster meat to the bowl and toss to coat evenly in lemon and truffle oil mixture .

To serve, open up the burrata using two forks, and then drizzling it with pesto. Top with a couple of slices of tomatoes. Then , add the lobster meat. Dot with garlic croutons. Finish with a pinch of sea salt and garnish with micro greens. This is one of the most decadent ways to enjoy lobster. For me, cold water lobster is alwasy the best. My all time favorite is Australian lobster, followed by Maine Lobster. *Serves 4*

For this recipe I use Maine Lobster, but Australian Lobster, would blow anybody socks off if you can find it!

It was a blast
having Ron in my
home kitchen.
I have to admit
I was kind of
intimidated to
share my rib recipe
after he shared his
"famous" ribs. The
man can cook!

#bbq baby back ribs
honey, scallions

2 **racks baby back pork ribs, about**
   4 pounds, each cut in half
1 **teaspoon garlic salt**
1 **teaspoon freshly ground black pepper**
1 **tablespoon brown sugar**
1 **teaspoon paprika**
1 **(12-ounce) bottle dark brown ale beer**
4 **cups ketchup**
1 **cup yellow onion, minced**
1 **cup honey**
½ **cup dry red wine**
2 **tablespoons fresh lemon juice**
2 **tablespoons Creole mustard**
2 **tablespoons brown sugar**
2 **tablespoons garlic, minced**
1 **tablespoon jalapeno, seeded and minced**
1 **tablespoon Worcestershire sauce**
1 **teaspoon hot pepper sauce**
1 **teaspoon kosher salt**
½ **teaspoon cayenne pepper**
½ **cup scallion, thinly sliced**

Combine garlic salt, black pepper, brown sugar, and paprika in a small mixing bowl and then rub mixture generously on ribs.

Place ribs in sealable container. Add beer to seasoned ribs, cover, and refrigerate for 8 hours or overnight. Remove the ribs from the bag and allow to come to room temperature. Preheat the grill to medium high.

Meanwhile, to make the sauce, whisk together the ketchup, onions, honey, red wine, lemon juice, mustard, brown sugar, garlic, jalapenos, Worcestershire, hot pepper sauce, salt, and cayenne in a large mixing bowl. Transfer ribs to grill and roast for 30 minutes covered without moving. Flip ribs over and begin basting every 15 minutes with barbecue sauce. Reduce heat to medium and continue to baste every 15 minutes for 2-2 ½ hours. Ribs are ready when they begin to peel away from the bone. To serve, sprinkle scallions over the top. *Serves 4*

Its NOT Good until it falls off the BONE

#torched black mission figs
whipped goat cheese and prosciutto

4 **black mission figs**
   sugar, for torching
½ **cup mild goat cheese**
1 **tablespoon heavy cream**
2 **oz prosciutto, thinly sliced**
¼ **cup garlic croutons, store bought (or home**
   made by dehydrating garlic bread)
¼ **teaspoon white truffle oil**
   kosher salt and freshly cracked black pepper
   micro greens for garnish

On a cleared work surface, cut each fig in half. Sprinkle sugar on the fig and torch it with a small creme brulee torch.

The top of the fig should resemble the top of a creme brulee. In a blender or handheld mixer, whip goat cheese and heavy cream to create a smoother, lighter consistency. Set aside.

When ready to plate, spoon and spread a spoonful of whipped goat cheese on serving dish, add torched fig, and top with thinly sliced prosciutto. Add crush garlic bread croutons and truffle oil. Sprinkle with a little bit of salt and pepper to desired taste. Garnish with micro greens. *Serves 2*

"I created this dish when fig season came around and couldn't resist putting these beautifully sweet figs with a salty counterpart like prosciutto. I also like that its accompanied by the decadence of whipped goat cheese. This dish is not only all about the flavor, but also textures."

This dish is an example of how we equally keep in mind flavor and texture.

#strawberry fields sundae

CRUST:
2 cups finely ground graham crackers (about 30 squares)
½ teaspoon ground cinnamon
1 stick unsalted butter, melted
FILLING:
1 pound cream cheese, 2 (8-ounce) blocks, softened
3 eggs
1 cup sugar
1 pint sour cream
1 tablespoon pure vanilla extract

Preheat the oven to 325 degrees F.
In a mixing bowl, combine the ingredients with a fork until evenly moistened. Lightly coat the bottom and sides of an 8-inch spring form pan with non-stick cooking spray. Pour the crumbs into the pan and, using the bottom of a measuring cup, press the crumbs down into the base and 1-inch up the sides. Refrigerate for 5 minutes.

FOR THE FILLING:
In the bowl of an electric mixer, beat the cream cheese on low speed for 1 minute until smooth and free of any lumps. Add the eggs, 1 at a time, and continue to beat slowly until combined. Gradually add sugar and beat until creamy, for 1 to 2 minutes. Add sour cream and vanilla. Occassionally scrape down the sides of the bowl and the beaters. The batter should be well-mixed and free of any lumps. Pour the filling in-to the crust-lined pan and smooth the top with a spatula. Set the cheesecake pan on a large piece of aluminum foil and fold up the sides around it. Place the cake pan in a large roasting pan. Pour boiling water into the roasting pan until the water is about halfway up the sides of the cheesecake pan; the foil will keep the water from seeping into the cheesecake. Bake for 45 minutes. The cheesecake should still jiggle (it will firm up after chilling).

WHIPPED CREAM:
2 cups heavy cream
½ cup sugar
½ teaspoon pure vanilla extract

DIRECTIONS:
Whip all the ingredients together until you form soft peaks.

You will need 2 cups of fresh strawberries, sliced for assembling the sundae. 2 pints Vanilla Ice Cream
To assemble: In a dessert bowl, using an ice cream scooper, make a base of cheesecake. Then, make another layer of vanilla ice cream. Stud with strawberry slices in and around cheesecake and ice cream. Repeat, this step three more times to make a gigantic sundae. Top with whipped cream and sprinkle with ex-tra cheese cake crust crumbs. (If you don't have any, you can crumble graham crackers and sprinkle them instead) Enjoy!

#condensed milk key lime pie

1 ½ **cups graham cracker crumbs**
½ **cup granulated sugar**
4 **tablespoons (½ stick butter) melted**
2 **(14-ounce) cans sweetened condensed milk plus**
  more for drizzling
1 **cup key lime or regular lime juice**
2 **whole large eggs**
1 **tablespoon lime zest**
1 **cup heavy whipping cream**
¼ **cup sugar**

Preheat the oven to 350 degrees F.

In a bowl, mix the graham cracker crumbs, sugar, and butter. Press the mixture firmly into a 9-inch pie pan, and bake until brown, about 15-20 minutes. Remove from the oven and allow to cool to room temperature before filling.

Lower the oven temperature to 325 degrees F.

In a separate bowl, combine the condensed milk, lime juice, and eggs. Whisk until well blended and place the filling in the pie shell. Bake in the oven for 15 minutes and allow to chill in the refrigerator for at least 2 hours.

Using an electric mixer, whip heavy cream on high adding the sugar to make stiff peaks. Top the chilled key lime pie with the whipped cream before serving and drizzle more condensed milk over the top. *Serves 8*

- #connected -

Condensed milk takes me to a happy place.

#balsamic panna cotta
raspberry reduction

4 **cups heavy cream**
½ **cup granulated sugar**
1 **tablespoon balsamic vinegar**
½ **teaspoon citric acid**
2 **cups fresh raspberries**
1 **cup sugar**
¼ **cup fresh lemon juice sugar for coating figs**

Stir together all the ingredients in a heavy-bottomed pot and bring to a simmer over medium heat. Divide mixture among 10 four-ounce ramekins. Cool, then cover tightly with plastic wrap and chill for at least 1 hour.

In a small sauce pan, combine raspberries, sugar, and lemon juice. Simmer for 15 minutes or until raspberries have macerated and reduced. When ready to serve, coat the inside of the split fig in sugar and torch with with a brulee torch. You can also set your oven to broil on high and broil the figs for a couple of minutes or just until sugar caramelizes.

For plating, spoon raspberry reduction on the bottom of a plate, then place panna cotta on top, and garnish with torched figs. *Serves 10*

"To take this plate over the top, I like to decorate it with micro greens, and gold coated white chocolate pearls. You can also buy dessert sauces for plating. The flavor profile of this dessert is a little outside the vanilla, chocolate, and strawberry comfort zone, but you'll be surprised how delicious this combination really is."

← **PHOTO** ↻

chefadrianne   🕐 3w

♥ 99 likes

chefadrianne Our balsamic panna cotta + raspberry reduction + torched black mission figs!!!
www.chefadriannes.com @eggandthecity #maximumflavor #miami #restaurants #bestof #chefs #chefadriannes

Are your amazing #cronuts coming back soon @chefadrianne 😳 💕 😊 #please #chefadrianne 🙌 🎪

Cannot wait to celebrate our anniversary with you on Sunday!!!

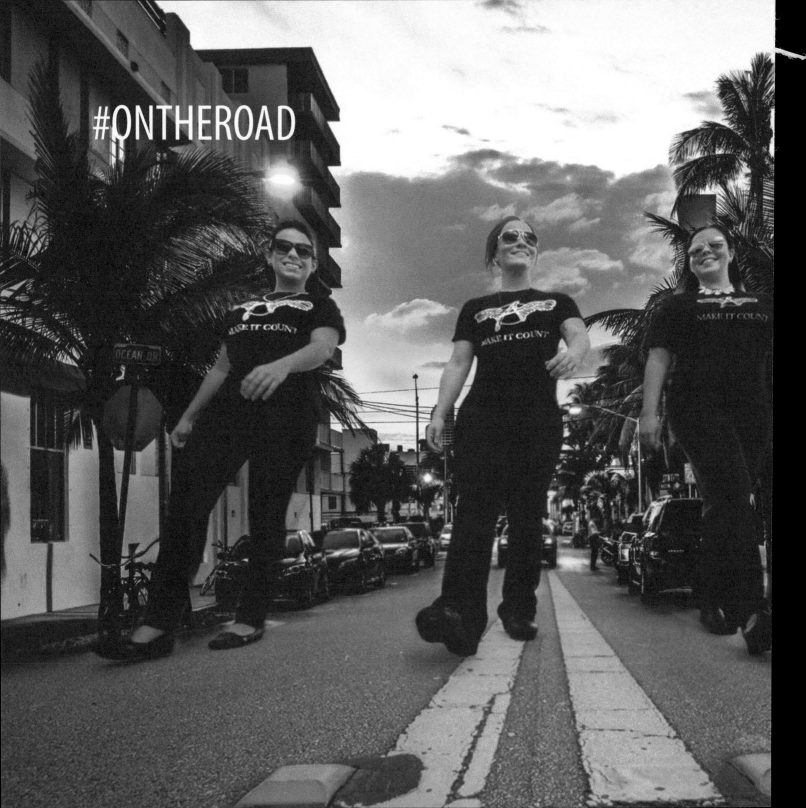

ONE BITE TO MAKE AN IMPACT

Totally random fact- I'm a full-fledged Disney fanatic, so you know the phrase "it's a Small World" holds a special place for me! Those 4 words just so happen to sum up one of the most fascinating effects that social media has on how we live our lives and connect with each other these days. I'm constantly reminded of this, in a very positive way, when I have an opportunity to get out into the community and take Maximum Flavor on the road. I've been lucky enough to be called upon to participate at several different events, both throughout the nation and close to home in South Florida, over the past few years. Each of these occasions is a memorable opportunity to put some faces to the wonderful messages I receive through my social networks. With as much time as I sometimes spend in the kitchen, the chance to meet some of my fans and followers personally outside of the restaurant environment gives me incredible satisfaction, often putting me in direct contact with those that I've already had the pleasure of being "digitally social" with in the past.

The different public interactions that I've been a part of usually range in size and scope, with audiences that are often anywhere from 500 to 3000. Every month is different- we might have a very quiet schedule for personal appearances one month and then be booked for 6-7 dates over the following 30 days after that. No matter how large or small the event, members of my staff and I have one primary goal in mind when we participate- bringing Maximum Flavor to the masses! The way we see it, we've got "one bite to make an impact" and expose a new audience to a taste of what we do at Chef Adrianne's.

Just as it does around the dinner table or at the restaurant, the food that we prepare and offer at these appearances is a socially bonding force that connects us to one another. While my staff usually takes care of providing the samples that we've prepared, I try to take the time to really try to meet as many of those people who are nice enough to show an interest and stop by. These moments can be special for a chef- the chance to interact directly with those who are sampling your work at the very moment they're doing so, and seeing for yourself what reaction it inspires! Of course, just having the chance to meet those who have been kind enough to offer support through social media, and at the same time make tons of new friends who are genuinely excited to try what we have to offer, truly does make my day and definitely provides me loads of motivation!

I think that one of the most fascinating aspects of practicing my art "live" and in front of an audience is that it produces a certain raw and visceral adrenaline that is really unique onto itself. The fusion of the intense but motivational pressure of having your every move watched, paired with the ability to receive that immediate feedback that pushes you to strive higher in your next course is special indeed. One particular event that I count as an all-time favorite, Chefs Up Front, really brings to life many of these awesome elements I am describing.

Chefs Up Front is coordinated and sponsored by an incredibly worthwhile organization, Flipany. Flipany is the lead Florida partner to the Share Our Strength program, which among other things, teaches children about the importance of the many health benefits in physical activity and nutrition. It's truly a pleasure for me to volunteer each year at Chefs Up Front, because the organization and its mission sincerely resonate with me. I also happen to really love the idea that one of the main attractions for guests is having their chosen chef literally "up front and center"; ten chefs are chosen and then the guests buy the tables assigned to the chef they select as their favorite. For example, if a guest was interested in experiencing some Maximum Flavor up close and personal, they would click on "Chef Adrianne Calvo- Table of ten", see my menu, and purchase it! All the money raised goes towards the program, which encourages underprivileged children to exercise regularly and to eat a diet consisting of fresh, whole foods instead of synthetically processed ones.

Perhaps the biggest motivator for me during Chefs Up Front is that sincere and very tangible energy in the room.. I'm typically about five feet away from my corresponding round table, allowing me to see the excitement and anticipation in the patrons' eyes. Some are reviewing the menu, others are making small talk among themselves, and then there's always that few that are blankly but intently staring at me as I'm going through last minute preparations! At this point I am usually counting my plates, making sure I have serving/plating spoons, gloves, and my array of squirt bottles. I take a deep breath, and off I go... Five courses must go out in a timely manner with no hiccups!

In my most recent opportunity to be a part of Chefs Up Front, I selected sliced blue fin tuna with a ponzu aioli and shaved jalapenos as my first course: a no-brainer for kick starting the palate! I also shaved radish and cucumber for more texture. I was pleased to see that after my audience sampled what I whipped up, Round One produced enthusiastic applause! This positive feedback put me totally "in the zone" – I began plating like clockwork and even began getting comfortable to the point of getting a little artsy with the sauces. Twelve minutes in, and the second course was ready to go out: a beautifully warming whipped sweet po-

maximum flavor to the masses!

tato bisque dusted with tiny, crispy bits of Spanish chorizo, and blue and gold tortilla strips. With this dish, my goal was a cozy, nurturing approach, but also with the objective of getting my guests excited about the textural elements of the dish. True, soup is soup, but when it's whipped, it's taken to a whole other level! In addition, most are familiar with chorizo, but not in the form of crispy dust. With that said, I'm proud to announce that Course Number Two was also a luscious success!

The following course is extremely special to me because it's one that we've been serving at Chef Adriannes for over six years now. It's been at the top of foodie lists, has been the subject of multiple blogs, rave reviews from local news channels, and overall labeled as a "must try"! In fact, all of our peeps on social media have put it in the prestigious "run don't walk" category when they suggest that people sample it! Yes, our famous Sweet Corn Tamalito, topped with grilled wild shrimp and served with a delicate but bursting-with- flavor lemon buerre blanc, was the next dish on the menu! I believe that what makes this delicacy so special is the symphony of flavors. Close your eyes and imagine a buttery, rich, corn pudding, very similar to cornbread, except its much lighter in texture and richer in taste. Now, imagine it topped with grilled wild shrimp and you start to get an idea of how mind blowing this whole dish is! The lemon buerre blanc came about due to my obsession with French cooking. I wanted to add a little bit of classic finesse to this dish, and the lemon buerre blanc was the perfect accumulation.

After the Sweet Corn Tamalito, the TKO (technical knock-out) was the last savory dish of the evening, which also happened to be one of our signature offerings at Chef Adrianne's, our 24-hour Braised Prime Beef Short Rib! When I was 17 years old, I read Ruth Reichl's book, "Tender at the Bone" and immediately fell in love with the tales she told about the great dishes that stood out in her life. This book really was the driving inspiration behind eventually creating a Maxi-

mum Flavor version of a short rib dish. I wanted to come up with something that people would talk about long after they tried it - something so delicious that it would embed a memory and have them perpetually craving it! There's so much love and attention that goes into making these short ribs that to this day, I genuinely feel a palpable excitement when it comes time to prepare them. Needless to say, I feel crazy butterflies when the oven timer begins to count down those last 30 seconds as I'm standing by breathless, waiting for the outcome. Are they falling off the bone? Are they too fatty? Are they caramelized enough? Did the color reach a deep, rich, reddish-brown? When a fork can lightly pull away the saucy meat from the bone, releasing that intoxicating aroma that makes you salivate - that's when I know I've conjured up a little bit of magic in my oven!

Following the short ribs (and a standing ovation!), I served our crazy delicious Dark Chocolate Nutella Croissant Bread Pudding with a Salted Caramel Crème Anglaise. I'm proud to say that it was the perfect conclusion to what was a 5 Course extravaganza of deliciousness, all put together in front of a very receptive and supportive live audience!

It's also gratifying to see that at many of the events in which multiple restaurants are represented, we are faced with the very good problem of running out of food! The Chef Adrianne's table is one where people make their way back for seconds because as they put it, "they just have to have one more" of what we've got! The excitement level also seeps right over into social media- I've often seen pics that I've taken with fans at an appearance pop up shortly after on Facebook or Instagram. By the same token, I've also been very pleased to receive both comments on my social networks as well as visits to the restaurant from those who tried one of our dishes at a public appearance and just had to come in for more!

#andouille sausage baked beans

1 large onion, diced
2 (16-ounce) cans pork and beans
3 tablespoons dijon mustard
½ cup pure maple syrup
1 tablespoon light brown sugar
4 tablespoons ketchup
1 teaspoon white vinegar
½ pound bacon strips, cut into 1/2-inch pieces
½ pound andouille sausage, cut into ¼ inch rings
½ teaspoon hot sauce
¼ cup green onions, thinly sliced

Preheat oven to 350 degrees F.

In a Dutch oven, mix onion, pork and beans, mustard, maple syrup, light brown sugar, ketchup, hot sauce and vinegar.

Top with the bacon pieces and sausage. Bake, covered, for 45 to 60 minutes. To serve, top with green onions. *Serves 6*

"I made this for the Nascar event at the Homestead Speedway to accompany a whole hog roast. I don't know what people were more excited about, the whole hog, or these pork and beans! My favorite is Andouille but feel free to interchange your favorite sausage!"

I made these beans for the Nascar event at the Homestead speedway to accompany a whole hog roast

The truffle Ponzu
aioli is the secret
weapon here.

#pan con lechon
truffle ponzu aioli

1 **(4 to 6-pound) pork shoulder, de-boned**
8 **cloves garlic**
1 **white onion, diced**
2 **bay leaves**
1 **teaspoon dried oregano**
1 **teaspoon cumin**
1 ½ **cups white vinegar**
½ **bunch cilantro, leaves picked**
 kosher salt and freshly ground black pepper
2 **cups lard**
2 **red onions, julienned**
2 **limes, juiced**
4 **(8-inch) pieces cuban bread**

TRUFFLE PONZU AIOLI:
1 **cup mayonnaise**
1 **tablespoon garlic, minced**
¼ **cup ponzu sauce**
1 **teaspoon white truffle oil**

With a knife, make a couple incisions in the pork shoulder and stud with the garlic cloves.
In a blender, puree onions, bay leaves, oregano, cumin, white vinegar, and cilantro. Season with salt and pepper. Pour the marinade over the pork shoulder, and refrigerate for at least 2 hours.

TRUFFLE PONZU AIOLI:
In a small mixing bowl, using a whisk, combine all the ingredients.

Preheat oven to 325 degrees F.
Place the pork shoulder in a roasting pan. Heat the lard, and pour over the top. Cover and bake 3 hours. Let the meat rest for 15 minutes. Slice thinly. Saute red onions and de glaze with lime juice. Assemble the sandwich by placing shredded bunches of pork and 2 to 3 tablespoons of the onion mixture on the bread. Then topping it with the truffle ponzu aioli. *Serves 4*

"I prepared this dish for Food Network's South Beach Food and Wine Festival's Target's Red Hot Night and I was so happy we had the longest line at the party! People couldn't get over the flavor! That's what its all about…Maximum Flavor."

February 24, 2013

With Chef Adrianne Calvo and Chef Adrianne at Red Hot Night - South Beach Wine and Food Festival.

Like · Comment · Share

 37 people like this.

U are the Best…Chef Adrianne..The Best Chef with a Big heart…Make it Count.. ♡
February 24, 2013 at 9:50pm · Like · 1

 Write a comment…

#elena ruz
done maximum flavor style

1 **brioche bun, buttered and toasted**
2 **ounce braised, pulled turkey breast**
1 **tablespoon whipped cornichon cream cheese**
1 **tablespoon strawberry preserves**
    white truffle oil

DIRECTIONS:
To assemble sandwich, spread cornichon cream cheese on the bottom piece of the brioche bun, top with pulled turkey, then top with a heaping spoon of strawberry preserves and a dab of truffle oil. Top with the other bun.

12 HOUR BRAISED TURKEY BREAST:
1 **turkey breast, boned to yield 2 halves**
½ **cup garlic cloves, peeled**
½ **pound carrots, peeled and diced**
½ **pound celery, trimmed and diced**
1 **large onion, sliced**
    several sage leaves
    stock or water as needed

Preheat the oven to 220 degrees F.
Place all the ingredients in a deep roasting pan and cover with aluminum foil. Check every 3 hours and adjust liquid with stock or water as needed until the 12 hours are complete. This can be done up to 3 days ahead and stored in the refrigerator.

WHIPPED CORNICHON CREAM CHEESE:
1 **cup cream cheese**
1 **tablespoon heavy cream**
4-6 **cornichon pickles**
In a food processor, blend all ingredients on high speed until well incorporated.

STRAWBERRY PRESERVES:
2 **cups sugar**
1 **large lemon, zested and juiced**
1 ½ **pints fresh strawberries, hulled and halved**

Combine the sugar, lemon zest, and lemon juice in a small saucepan and cook over low heat for 10-12 minutes, until the sugar is dissolved. Add the strawberries and continue to cook over low heat for 20 minutes, until the strawberries release some of their juices and the mixture boils slowly. Pour carefully into 2 pint canning jars and either seal or keep refrigerated. *Serves 1*

I'm not just saying this because its my recipe, but this is the best, fried chicken biscuit I've ever had. The crunch from the slaw and the guidance from the honey truffle mayo... wow

#fried chicken biscuit
honey truffle mayo and slaw

1 **garlic clove, finely grated**
½ **cup mayonnaise**
1 **tablespoon honey**
½ **teaspoon white truffle oil**
1 **teaspoon louisiana-style hot pepper sauce**
½ **small red onion, thinly sliced**
1 **jalapeño, thinly sliced**
4 **cups thinly sliced cabbage**
½ **up bread-and-butter pickle slices plus**
¼ **cup pickle juice**
2 **cups all-purpose flour**
1 **tablespoon ground black pepper**
½ **teaspoon kosher salt**
1 **cup buttermilk**
2 **8-ounce skinless, boneless chicken breasts, halved crosswise, peanut or vegetable oil (for frying)**
4 **buttermilk biscuits, homemade**
2 **tablespoons unsalted butter, room temperature**

HONEY TRUFFLE MAYO AND SLAW:
Mix garlic, mayonnaise, honey, truffle oil, and hot pepper sauce in a small bowl; cover and chill. Toss onion, jalapeño, cabbage, pickles, and pickle juice in a large bowl to combine; cover and chill.

FRIED CHICKEN AND ASSEMBLY:
Whisk flour, pepper, and salt in a bowl. Pour buttermilk into another shallow bowl. Working with 1 piece at a time, dredge chicken in flour mixture, shaking off excess. Dip in buttermilk, allowing excess to drip back into bowl. Dredge again in flour mixture, shaking off excess.

Pour oil into a large heavy skillet to a depth of 1/2-inch. Prop deep-fry thermometer in oil so bulb is submerged. Heat over medium high heat until thermometer registers 350°.

Fry chicken until golden brown and cooked through, about 3 minutes per side. Transfer to a wire rack. Spread butter on the biscuits. Spread with mayo. Build sandwiches with biscuit, chicken, and cabbage slaw. *Serves 4*

Chef Adrianne
September 28, 2013

Hard work pays off. So happy people enjoyed our Fried Chicken!!! We Won Cluck Miami!!!!

🏷 Tag Photo   ♀ Add Location   ✏ Edit

Like · Comment · Share

👍   Top Comments ▾
and 259 others like this.

congratulations - yu continue to amaze!
Like · Reply · September 29, 2013 at 9:36pm

#crispy goat cheese
fig preserve, prosciutto, balsamic, and white truffle

 canola oil, for frying
¼ **cup cornstarch**
¾ **cup all-purpose flour**
1 **cup club soda**
1 **10-ounce log of fresh goat cheese**
3 **cups panko bread crumbs**
 kosher salt
1 **large egg, lightly beaten**
1 **cup fig preserves, store bought or homemade**
¼ **cup balsamic glaze**
8 **slices prosciutto, thin**
1 **teaspoon white truffle oil**

Cut the goat cheese log into 16 pieces and roll each piece into a ball. Refrigerate the balls on a wax paper–lined baking sheet until firm, about 20 minutes.

In a bowl, whisk the egg and club soda. Gradually whisk in the flour and cornstarch and season with salt.

Spread the panko in a shallow bowl. Dip the goat cheese balls in the egg batter, then dredge in the panko.

Coat the balls again in egg batter and panko. Return them to the baking sheet and freeze just until firm, about 20-25 minutes. In a large saucepan, heat 2 inches of canola oil to 375°. Working in batches, fry the cheese balls over high heat, turning occasionally, until golden and crisp, about 2 minutes.

Using a slotted spoon, transfer the balls to a paper towel–lined plate.

To serve, spoon fig preserves on bottom of a plate, then add a small nest of prosciutto, place a fried goat cheese ball in center of each prosciutto nest. Drizzle with balsamic and truffle. *Serves 4*

" This dish exemplifies what I mean by seducing all parts of the palate. When we first started running this as a special only on Friday nights at the restaurant, it was chaos! We couldn't make enough balls, lol! Every single table would order them, and once they got to the table, 10 minutes later, they'd order another round. A couple months later, they made it to our menu. Five years later, the craze has not died down over these balls! "

This dish exemplifies what I mean by seducing all parts of the palate.

#white cheddar grits

4 ½ cups water, plus more if needed
1 cup white grits
¾ cup sharp white-cheddar cheese, grated
1 ½ teaspoons kosher salt
1/8 teaspoon cayenne pepper

Bring water to a boil in a medium pot.

Whisking constantly, slowly add grits to water and cook until mixture starts to thicken, about 1 minute.

Reduce heat to medium-low, and simmer gently, stirring occasionally, until grits are smooth about 25-30 minutes.

Add cheese, salt, and cayenne, and stir just until cheese melts. Serve immediately.

Adding cheese to grits really takes them to another level of richness. You can really use any cheese for this recipe.

Parmesan, brie, swiss, you name it, its interchangeable. This is one of the greatest parts of cooking. *Serves 4*

Adding cheese to grits really takes them to another level of richness. You can use any cheese for this recipe. Parmesan, brie, swiss, you name it, its interchangeable. (one of the greatest parts of cooking)

#the ultimate coleslaw

1 **cup mayonnaise**
1 **tablespoon dijon mustard**
½ **lemon, juiced**
½ **teaspoon worcestershire sauce**
¼ **teaspoon tabasco sauce**
¼ **teaspoon celery seed kosher salt and**
   freshly ground black pepper
1 **tablespoon red wine vinegar**
1 **tablespoon sugar**
1 **store-bought bag shredded slaw mix (counting**
   red and green cabbage and carrots

In a large bowl, mix together the dressing in-gredients. Add the shredded slaw mix and toss until combined.

In this recipe, what makes this coleslaw amaz-ing is the kick from the celery seed. It's definetly a must! *Serves 6*

- #on the road -

This coleslaw can be made and stored up to 2 days in advance. But I love this recipe made fresh so its served with the vegetables still crunchy!

The secret to sauteing
fantastic onions is
to cook them in butter
over medium heat so
their natural sugars
release at the perfect
time.

#short rib sliders

4 **brioche buns, buttered and warmed**
16 **ounce braised shortrib, fully cooked**
   (could be left-overs), use your favorite braised
   shortrib recipe
16 **ounce cipollini onions, sauteed until**
   translucent (if you can't find cipollni's, sweet
   yellow onions may be used)
4 **ounce mild goat cheese, room temperature,**
   spreadable
2 **ounce balsamic vinegar**

Warm buns and butter them.
To assemble, spread a spoonful of goat cheese on bottom half of bun. Layer on top, the shortrib, followed by the onion and balsamic vinegar. Serve warm. *Serves 4*

"I made these at "The Grind" Burger battle, and they had everybody going crazy over them! They melt in your mouth. The sauteed onions with balsamic are irresistible!."

#prime beef omakase

3 inches fresh ginger root, minced
¼ cup tamari dark soy sauce
¼ cup garlic, minced
¼ cup brown sugar
2 tablespoons canola oil
1 teaspoon toasted sesame oil
1 (¼pounds) prime beef tenderloin, 1 ½ inches
   thick steak seasoning blend or fresh ground
   black pepper
1 package, minimum 40 count,
8-inch bamboo skewers
1 cup mayonnaise
1 tablespoon horseradish
1 teaspoon honey
1 teaspoon soy sauce

HORSERADISH AIOLI:
In a small mixing bowl, combine all ingredients. I like to serve this appetizer with pickled radishes (such as Daikon and crispy lotus root for contrast in flavors and textures. In a mixing bowl, using a whisk combine ginger, garlic, sugar, soy sauce , canola oil and sesame oil to make a marinade.

Then pour marinade into a shallow dish for the beef. Cut raw meat against the grain in thin strips. Thread strips on to skewers.

Set into the marinade. Season with steak seasoning. In a hot skillet or grill, cook beef 1-2 minutes on each side. *Serves 6*

" It was a huge hit at Share Our Strength's Taste of the Nation event! "

- #on the road -

The pop in this recipe
comes from the crispy
lotus root.

#whipped sweet potatoes

4 **large sweet potatoes, scrubbed**
1 **tablespoon canola oil**
  kosher salt and freshly ground black pepper
2 **cups heavy cream**
½ **teaspoon ground cinnamon**
2 **tablespoons brown sugar**
1 **tablespoon unsalted butter**

Preheat the oven to 350 degrees F.

Prick the sweet potatoes all over with a fork, drizzle with oil and season with salt and pepper. Put them in a roasting pan and roast for 45 minutes until they are soft.

Remove the pan from the oven. In a small sauce pot, over low heat, heat the cream. When the potatoes are cool enough to handle, scoop the flesh into the bowl of a food processor.

Season with salt, cinnamon and brown sugar. Add cream and 1 tablespoon of butter and puree until super smooth. *Serves 10*

I serve these at the restaurant with our 24 hour braised short Ribs
the combination of sweet and savory take your palate for a joyride.
Try these out next Thanksgiving as opposed to the standard sweet potato
casserole your guests will thank you.

Basic Training

#cacio e pepe

6 ounces parpadelle pasta
3 tablespoons unsalted butter, cubed, divided
1 teaspoon freshly cracked black pepper
1 cup finely grated grana padano or parmesan
1/3 cup finely grated pecorino
1 teaspoon white truffle oil
  kosher salt

Bring 3 quarts water to a boil in a 5 quart pot. Season with salt; add pasta and cook, stirring occasionally, until about 1-2 minutes before tender.

Drain, reserving 3/4 cup pasta cooking water. In the meantime, melt 2 tablespoons butter in a large heavy skillet over medium heat. Add pepper and cook, swirling pan, until toasted, about 1 minute. Add 1/2 cup reserved pasta water to skillet and bring to a simmer.

Add pasta and remaining butter. Reduce heat to low and add Grana Padano, stirring and tossing with tongs until melted. Remove pan from heat; add Pecorino, stirring and tossing until cheese melts, sauce coats the pasta, and pasta is al dente.

Transfer pasta to warm bowls, drizzle with truffle oil, and serve. *Serves 2*

"This might just be my all time favorite pasta dish. Its personifies minimalist..literally means cheese and pepper. Astonishing really, that there's no garlic in this authentic Italian recipe. Most people think mac and cheese for comfort food, I think cacio e pepe."

I saw this dish for the first time on Anthony Bourdain's show, No Reservations and became completely infatuated with Rome's passion for this particular Pasta.

#sweet and spicy shrimp

14 jumbo shrimp, cleaned and de veined
   extra-virgin olive oil, about
½ cup for brushing
   kosher salt and fresh black pepper
¼ cup sweet chili sauce
1 teaspoon garlic, minced
¼ cup mayonnaise

Preheat griddle or grill pan over high heat.
Butterfly shrimp by slicing almost through lengthwise.
Brush shrimps with oil, season with salt and pepper and grill 2 minutes on each side, until the shrimp is pink and opaque.
To make the sauce, using a mixing bowl, whisk together sweet chili, garlic, and mayonnaise until smooth.
When ready to serve, warm up the sauce in a small sauté pan over medium heat. Toss shrimp in sauce and serve immediately. *Serves 2*

" This appetizer has been a guest favorite for more than seven years. It's been one of the longest running menu items at Chef Adrianne's and still continues to amaze our patrons just as much as it did when we first opened. "

Talk about an easy recipe that packs a punch!

This dish is so beautiful, enticing to the eye, and it come with an unexpected flavor from an oyster. Something really out of the box.

#crispy cornmeal crusted oysters
mango and spicy horseradish

30 shucked oysters, patted dry
   (reserve shells for plating)
   kosher salt and freshly ground pepper
2 cups yellow cornmeal
   canola oil for frying
1 ripe mango, pitted and diced
1 tablespoon lemon juice
1 tablespoon chipotle puree
1 tablespoon honey
   kosher salt and pepper
2 tablespoons prepared horseradish
¼ teaspoon cayenne pepper
1 jalapeno , thinly sliced
¼ cup chives, minced

Season oysters with salt and pepper. Place cornmeal in a medium bowl and season with salt and pepper. Dredge each oyster into the cornmeal and tap off any excess. Heat 1 inch of oil in a large frying pan over medium high heat. Fry oysters in batches until golden brown on both sides, about 1 minute on each side.

MANGO SAUCE:
Place all ingredients in a blender and puree until smooth. Serve immediate or store airtight in refrigerator for up to 2 days.

SPICY HORSERADISH:
In a small mixing bowl, combine horseradish and cayenne to achieve a red color.

For plating, using the reserved oyster shell (make sure it's cleaned and rinsed) place a spoonful of mango puree in the center of the shell. Add the fried oyster. Top with horseradish, and one jalapeno slice on each. Finish with sprinkling minced chives over the top. *Serves 6*

"This dish is so beautiful, enticing to the eye, and so delicious at the same time… I'm sure it will be the talk of the town for time to come, if you make these at your next dinner party or BBQ!"

#sweet corn tamalito

1 cup milk
1/3 cup yellow cornmeal
½ teaspoon kosher salt
1 cup canned corn kernels, drained
2 large eggs, lightly beaten
2 tablespoons butter, cut in small pieces

Preheat the oven to 400 degrees F.

In a medium saucepan, whisk together the milk, cornmeal, and salt.

Cook over medium-high heat, stirring constantly, until mixture has thickened, about 6-7 minutes.

Temper the eggs by slowly whisking some of the hot milk mixture into the beaten eggs.

Stir the tempered eggs into the milk mixture. Pour the mixture into a 1-quart baking dish. Top with pieces of butter. Bake for 25 to 30 minutes or until center is set.

Remove from the oven and serve immediately.
Serves 4

" I serve this at the restaurant with grilled shrimp, chipotle, scallions, and a garlic cream. But this is a great side dish for almost anything. Try it with grilled chicken, pork chops, and even fish! "

I have a real soft spot for this dish. When I think of Chef Adrianne's Vineyard Restaurant and Wine Bar, our tamalito comes to mind. ♡

Consuming our Dark Chocolate Nutella Croissant Bread Pudding may cause large bouts of euphoria and happiness.

#dark chocolate nutella croissant bread pudding

3 **extra-large whole eggs**
8 **extra-large egg yolks**
5 **cups half-and-half**
1 ½ **cups sugar**
1 ½ **teaspoons pure vanilla extract**
½ **teaspoon kosher salt**
6 **croissants, preferably stale**
1 **cup semi-sweet chocolate chips**
1 **cup nutella®**

Preheat the oven to 350 degrees F.

In a medium bowl, whisk together the whole eggs, egg yolks, half-and-half, sugar, salt, and vanilla. Set the custard mixture aside. Slice the croissants in half horizontally. In a 10 by 15 by 2 1/2-inch oval baking dish, distribute the bottoms of the sliced croissants, then add the chocolate chips and nutella, then add the tops of the croissant. Pour the custard over the croissants and allow to soak for 10 minutes, pressing down gently.

Place the pan in a larger one filled with 1-inch of hot water. Cover the larger pan with aluminum foil, tenting the foil so it doesn't touch the pudding. Cut a few holes in the foil to allow steam to let out. Bake for 45 minutes. Uncover and bake for 40 to 45 more minutes or until the pudding puffs up and the custard is set. Remove from the oven and cool slightly. Serve warm or at room temperature. At the restaurant, we serve it with vanilla ice cream. *Serves 8*

Chef Adrianne Calvo
May 8, 2013

Our Dark Chocolate Nutella Croissant Bread Pudding right out of the oven!!!
www.chefadriannes.com

Tag Photo · Add Location · Edit

Like · Comment · Stop Notifications · Share

and 72 others **like this.**

5 shares

· 15 mutual friends
Obscenely delicious!
May 9, 2013 at 12:17am · Like

· 5 mutual friends
OMGoodness....this is hands down the BEST!
May 9, 2013 at 6:25am · Like

OMG!
May 9, 2013 at 7:06am · Like

#DARKDINING

A NIGHT MADE FOR SOCIAL MEDIA

Our extraordinary "Dark Dining" nights have always represented an interesting contrast- the dimly lit environment we create provides a very intimate feel. Each of these events is virtually dripping with "social"! I believe we have a natural tendency as social beings to want to share whatever catches our eye or stands out, and I've seen this proven time and time again over our last 6 years of hosting these unique events at Chef Adrianne's.

Now granted, eating in the dark in South Florida-where there seems to be a power outage without rhyme or reason a couple of times a day- isn't exactly new and note worthy! What is a little bit out of the norm is when the darkness is actually voluntary, and when everyone around you is enjoying a meal in the same unusual way.

A typical Dark Dining "social cycle" launches well before that first candle is lit. It seems that from the moment the date of the next event is first announced on my social media accounts, the momentum begins building quickly. Of course, in the Social Media age, "quickly"= 60 seconds or less! This brief window of time following the "big reveal" is very exciting for me and usually a pretty accurate indicator of how much attention that Dark Dining night will generate. It's always gratifying to see the raw and unfiltered emotion of both those who've already experienced one of these memorable nights, in addition to the ones who've been waiting "for years to try this", as many a Dark Dining novice has exclaimed.

The actual occasion of each Dark Dining-themed evening is also the subject of a ton of buzz and coverage in the social media arena, with many of our guests beginning to digitally document their experience from the moment they arrive! I've been pleasantly surprised on more than one occasion to find everything from the exterior of the restaurant, to the Dark Dining mask for the evening displayed on someone's Twitter, Facebook, or Instagram account. This usually leads to a piquing curiosity of the many within that person's own social circles; eventually, you have folks with two or three degrees of separation from the original commenter contributing to the level of anticipation as well! In this way, I would say that social media definitely intensifies the popularity and profile of both Chef Adrianne's and our unique twist on the Dark Dining phenomenon.

There's also something about the whole idea of sharing a meal with others under "Dark Dining" conditions that actually seems to enhance the level and focus of social interaction. Since their eyes are temporarily shielded from all of the typical distractions that you find on any given night at the res-

taurant, Dark Dining customers seem to be more honed in to who they're there with and with sharing the newness and exciting uncertainty of the whole experience with them. The food, the company around them, as well as the captivating ambiance more often than not seems to become the focal point of many of the conversations I've observed.

I can't forget to mention that I get in on the fun during these special, crazy nights too. A "normal" evening (if there is such a thing!) at Chef Adrianne's usually finds me in my second home, the kitchen. A Dark Dining event

"flips the script" in many ways though, and one example of that is me taking on the role of hostess for the night, interacting with my guests tons more than I normally have the pleasure of doing. I grab a mic and kind of serve as the "seeing eye chef", leading my guests through their Maximum Flavor courses, Dark Dining style! After dessert, that intermingling and connecting continues when I have the opportunity to take loads of pics with anyone who's interested. A couple of minutes later, when the notifications of those shots hitting social media start blowing up my phone, I know the Dark Dining social cycle has come full circle!

One particular Dark Dining event that truly took the entire concept to another level was our special "Eyes Wide Shut" themed night in September of 2013. As you'll come to learn further in this book, my staff and I have made the renowned St. Jude Children's Hospital in Memphis, Tennessee our adopted charitable cause for many years. While we make it a point to pay a personal visit annually to their facility, the opportunity also arose to significantly raise awareness in our home base of South Florida by leveraging the amazing popularity of the Dark Dining phenomenon. A special fundraising edition of Dark Dining, the first to ever be hosted outside of Chef Adrianne's, was carefully and painstakingly planned for a full year.

The goal from the jump was to put together an experience that was going to provide the guests with complete sensory overload in every way; when you consider that the final itinerary included amazing contortionists and stunning mermaids in a pool at a very elegant venue, I'd say we more or less nailed it! Needless to say, with as much eye and taste bud candy as the Eyes Wide Shut version of Dark Dining offered, it ended up as a perfect "made for social media" night! I'm very proud to say the event got so much traction through the tons of pictures and comments posted that to this day, typing "#darkdining" basically lets you digitally relive the magic!

Of course, with Dark Dining having originated in Europe, there's a whole level of awareness about it in places way beyond our South Florida location! I'm pleased to say that the Maximum Flavor version of Dark Dining, thanks to a little digital social networking, has started to get the attention of foodies on a global level! It never ceases to amaze me how channels such as Facebook, Twitter, and Instagram allow me to connect and interact with those halfway (or more!) around the world about Chef Adrianne's and the entire experience. The combination of the incredible reach of those platforms and the dedication that our awesome fans show in spreading the word to everyone they know about this unique way of sharing a meal has really brought about some eye-opening results; I've been humbled and pleasantly surprised on more than one occasion by "tweets" and postings from fans abroad letting me know that they plan to make a visit to Chef Adrianne's a definitive part of their South Florida vacation itinerary, and even a couple that want to plan a trip around the next Dark Dining night!

#darkdining
recipe index

What is very interesting about this recipe, is you cannot tell the difference between watermelon and cucumber on your palette. Maybe that's because watermelon is actually a cucumber!

#three melon greek salad
champagne mustard vinaigrette

½ cup red onion, thinly sliced
1 cup seedless watermelon, cubed
1 cup honey dew melon, cubed
1 cup cantaloupe, cubed
1 cup cucumber, seeded and cubed
½ cup feta cheese, crumbled
1/3 cup black olives, pitted and halved
1 1/3 tablespoons extra virgin olive oil
1 tablespoon champagne vinegar
1 teaspoon lemon juice
1 teaspoon honey
kosher salt and freshly ground black pepper
chives, for garnish

In small mixing bowl, whisk together olive oil, vinegar, lemon juice, honey, & salt and pepper to taste. Mix vigorously until well combined. In a large mixing bowl, add the remaining ingredients and toss.

Allow to sit for 15 minutes for flavors to come together. Add the dressing to the bowl but reserve a spoonful for garnishing later if desired. Toss with large spoons being careful not to bruise the melons.

You can serve this salad right away but it's best when refrigerated for 30 minutes to 1 hour. To serve, spoon in the center of a plate, drizzle with extra dressing, and garnish with a chive. Champagne Mustard Vinaigrette **Serves 4**

#pretzel crusted crab cake
beer and spicy brown mustard sauce

1   tablespoon canola oil
¾ cup finely diced onion
½ cup finely diced celery
1   cup unsalted butter, softened
1   cup mayonnaise
2   pounds lump crab meat, picked clean of
    all shell and cartilage
3   tablespoons minced fresh chives
1   teaspoon worcestershire sauce
2   teaspoons old bay seasoning
1   teaspoon ketchup
    pinch of cayenne pepper
2   large eggs
1   bag of hard pretzels, crushed until pulverized
    canola oil for frying
1   cup dark beer
½ cup honey
1/3 cup spicy brown mustard
1   tablespoon light soy sauce

Heat oil in a small saute pan over medium heat. Add onion and celery and saute vegetables for about 5 minutes, or until they are translucent. Remove onion and celery and drain off.

Combine butter and mayonnaise in a large mixing bowl. Using a handheld electric mixer or a wooden spoon, beat until mixture is well blended and very smooth. Fold in crab meat, chives, Old Bay, ketchup, and cayenne along with reserved onions and celery.

Cover and refrigerate crab cake mixture for 2-3 hours to chill. In a mixing bowl, whisk eggs. In another mixing bowl, place pulverized pretzel crumbs. Pull out crab mix from the refrigerator and make tablespoon sized spheres using the palm of your hands. Dip into pretzel bowl to cover, then into egg wash, and then into pretzel once again. Repeat for all the crab mixture.

Meanwhile heat a tall sauce pot filled halfway with canola oil to medium high heat. Fry pretzel crusted crab cake spheres for 2-3 minutes until golden and warmed through. Place on paper towel to drain.

BEER AND SPICY BROWN MUSTARD SAUCE:
In a small sauté pan, whisk together all ingredients and bring to a   simmer. Cook for 3-4 minutes.

To serve, spoon sauce on plate and add a little extra pulverized pretzel if you'd like. Top with the crab cake and enjoy warm. **Serves 4**

"I think this is a fun combination because pretzels always go with mustard so this is like elevating that combination to a whole other level."

Roxanne Vargas @RoxyNBC6 · Jul 15
#selfie @chefadrianne #darkdining 100% of tonight's event will benefit @LiveLikeBella #makeitcount #livelikebella pic.twitter.com/sPPPUKlyK1

Expand

Roxanne Vargas @RoxyNBC6 · Jul 15
#MakeItCount let's see (or not)what @ChefAdrianne has in store for a special #DarkDining to benefit @LiveLikeBella pic.twitter.com/9wy9R05kcV

Chef Adrianne's Dark Dining

RETWEET 1   FAVORITES 3

4:36 PM - 15 Jul 2014 · Details   Flag media

It is amazing and humbling to learn where our food comes from. Whether it be land or sea, there's so much to eat!

#scallop on the half shell
frozen coconut milk, lime, black lava salt

8 ounce bay scallops
½ cup coconut milk, unsweetened
1 lime, juiced
1 lime, wedges for garnish
1 teaspoon cilantro, minced
   hot sauce, optional
   black lava salt

Place coconut milk in a disposable container and freeze for 4 hours or overnight.
Remove side muscle from the scallop keeping the actual scallop in the shell. Rinse thoroughly with cold water and pat dry.
Place scallops on the shell on a clean work surface. Add a splash of lime to each scallop and let marinate for 5-7 minutes.
Top each scallop with a light sprinkle of cilantro and splash of hot sauce.
When ready to serve, top each scallop with about a teaspoon's worth of frozen coconut milk. Sprinkle with black lava salt and garnish with a thin lime wedge.
Serve very cold. **Serves 2**

"This dish is very versatile because all the parts of the recipe can be adjusted to your own palette. For example, if you like it spicier, simply add more hot sauce."

Ive also done this dish with fresh frozen lemonade, and it also causes Palette fireworks!

- #dark dining -

Warning: consuming this kind of caviar sends strong euphoric sensations through your body, that of luxurious happiness... Love and other drugs.

#classic caviar service
russian ossetra, brioche toast points

4 **ounces russian ossetra caviar**
2 **hard-boiled eggs**
1 **small red onion, minced**
1 **tablespoon chives, minced**
8 **brioche toast points**
  white truffle oil
  micro greens, for garnish

Preheat the oven to 400 degrees F.

To make toast points, cut a small piece of a brioche loaf into small squares ¼ inch thick and place on a baking sheet. Bake for 3-4 minutes to toast a bit then allow to cool at room temperature.
For the eggs, pass the yolks through a small fine sieve and mince the whites.

To serve, drizzle white truffle oil lightly on each toast point. Top with yolks on one half, whites on the other. Then layer with red onion and top with a small spoonful of caviar. Add chives and micro greens for garnish. ***Serves 4***

#patatas bravas
sriracha tomato and garlic aioli

4 **medium potatoes**
  kosher salt to taste
2 **cups spanish olive oil for frying**
½ **spanish onion, minced**
1 **(16 ounce) can of tomato sauce**
1 ½ **teaspoon mustard**
1 **teaspoon sriracha hot sauce**
1 **teaspoon sweet spanish paprika**
3/4 **cup mayonnaise**
4 **cloves garlic, minced**
¼ **cup lemon juice**
3/4 **teaspoon kosher salt**
½ **teaspoon ground black pepper**
  chives, minced for garnish

Peel the potatoes. Cut potatoes into 1/2" chunks as follows: lengthwise, then cut it lengthwise again. You should have four long pieces. Now, cut each of those pieces into 3-4 pieces, cutting crosswise. This should give you nice bit-sized pieces. Sprinkle with kosher salt.

Pour olive oil in a large, heavy bottom frying pan. Heat the oil on medium high until hot. Fry the potatoes for about 10-12 minutes. Once the potatoes are fried, use a slotted spoon to remove and set them aside to drain.

Using a small 8-inch frying pan, put 1, to 2 tablespoons of the olive oil in the pan. Heat over medium heat. Add the onion and sauté for 5 minutes until translucent. Pour tomato sauce into the pan and "saute" the tomato sauce for 5 more minutes. Turn heat down and add the mustard, stirring well. Finally, add the Sriracha and paprika. Taste the sauce and adjust as necessary with salt. Pour mixture in a blender and mix to make a velvety tomato sauce.

Next, using a mixing bowl, whisk together mayonnaise, garlic, lemon juice, salt and pepper.

Place the potatoes on a plate and dot with sriracha tomato sauce alternating with garlic aioli. Garnish with extra Spanish paprika and chives.

Serves 6

We've done different areas of Spain for a few Dark Dinings, and our guests are alway ecstatic about these potatoes

This recipe was actually ispired by Julia Child and her love for French cookery.

#pan seared mahi mahi
lemon parsley butter

6 **(6-8 ounce) portions mahi**
  mahi fillets, skinned
1 **teaspoon garlic salt**
1 **teaspoon paprika**
1 **teaspoon freshly ground black pepper**
1 **cup dry white wine**
½ **cup lemon juice**
2 **tablespoons minced garlic**
1 **tablespoon shallot, minced**
1 **tablespoon fresh parsley, minced**
1 **teaspoon kosher salt**
¼ **teaspoon black pepper**
1 **dash worcestershire sauce**
1 **dash hot pepper sauce**
1 **cup butter, room temperature**
  butter for pan searing

Heat a large skillet over high heat. Add the wine, lemon juice, garlic, and shallots. Cook for 4 minutes. Stir in the parsley, salt, pepper, Worcestershire, and hot sauce and simmer for 1-2 minutes. Over low heat, whisk in the butter a few pieces at a time.

Continue whisking until all of the butter is incorporated into the sauce. Serve immediately or keep warm until ready to use. In small bowl, combine garlic salt, pepper, and paprika. Season fish fillets with seasoning blend. Preheat oven to 400 degrees F. In an oven proof heavy skillet, add enough butter to coat the bottom. Heat to medium high.

Gently, place seasoned side of fillet onto the hot buttered skillet. Sear for 2 minutes being careful not to move around in the pan. Using a spatula, turn over. Repeat for all fillets. Once all fillets are seared on seasoned side, place pan with fillets in the oven and cook for 7 minutes or until cooked through. To serve, place a fish fillet on center of plate and spoon sauce over the top.

Serves 6

#olive oil and chablis poached cobia
green olives, capers, toasted almonds

2 (8 ounce) cobia fillets, skinned, boned
½ cup extra virgin olive oil
½ cup chablis wine
1 tablespoon lemon juice, fresh
1 tablespoon spanish olives, sliced, pitted
1 tablespoon capers
1 tablespoon almond slivers, toasted
sea salt and freshly ground black pepper

Preheat the oven to 300 degrees F.

In a baking dish, place cobia fillets. Add olive oil, Chablis wine, and lemon juice. Make sure the fish fillets are submerged in liquid.

Add olives and capers. Cover tightly with aluminum foil and bake in preheated oven for 10-12 minutes.

During that cooking time, in a separate baking sheet, toast almond slivers to bring out the natural flavorful oils from the nuts.

To serve, using a fish spatula, remove fillets from baking dish, reserving liquid. Place fish fillet in the center of the plate and spoon reserved cooking liquid from the baking dish over the fish. Top with toasted almonds. Adjust seasoning to your taste with sea salt and pepper.

Serves 2

Sometimes the most simple recipes are the most delicious.

The almonds can be substituted for pecans, hazelnuts, or walnuts even pistachios would be equally delicious.

#crispy pork wonton
scallion and garlic chili paste

1 **(16 ounce) pork tenderloin, cut into 1 inch cubes**
1 **tablespoon minced fresh ginger root**
4 **cloves garlic, crushed**
1 **green onion, chopped**
1 **tablespoon fresh lime juice**
¼ **teaspoon crushed red pepper flakes**
1 **tablespoon sesame oil**
1 **teaspoon light soy sauce**
   ground black pepper to taste
1 **(12 ounce) package square wonton wrappers**
1 **egg white, beaten**
2 **quarts canola oil for frying**
   green onion, sliced diagonal for serving
   garlic chili paste, for serving

Combine the pork, ginger, garlic, green onion, lime juice, crushed red pepper, sesame oil, and soy sauce in a food processor.

Season mixture with pepper. Pulse until pork is minced to the consistency of ground beef. Separate the wonton wrappers and lay them out on a clean work surface.

Spoon 1 tablespoon of the pork mixture into the center of each wrapper. Moisten the edges of the wonton wrappers with water, fold over the filling to form a triangle, and press tightly together to seal.

Brush each wonton with egg white. Pour the canola oil into a large pot and heat to medium high heat or 375 degrees F.

Carefully drop wontons into the hot oil and cook until golden brown for about 4- 5 minutes. Remove from oil and onto paper towels to drain. Serve with garlic chili paste and scallions.

Serves 8

" I love garlic chili paste, but if it's difficult to find, sweet chili sauce is also a great alternative and can be found in most supermarkets."

#whipped ricotta crostini
country ham, black pepper honey

1 ciabatta loaf, sliced ¼ inch thick
1 cup ricotta cheese
1 teaspoon sugar
½ teaspoon garlic salt
¼ cup heavy cream
¼ cup honey
½ teaspoon freshly ground black pepper
1 (5-7 pound) ham, spiraled and smoked
1 cup honey
1 cup dijon mustard
½ cup brown sugar

Preheat the oven to 375 degree F.

In a small mixing bowl, whisk together honey, dijon mustard, and brown sugar. Spread the mixture evenly over the ham. Bake the ham for 45-55 minutes basting it every 10-15 minutes with pan juices.

Meanwhile, on a cookie sheet, arrange the ciabatta slices and bakes for 7-10 minutes, or until they toast and begin to turn golden.

Add ricotta, sugar, garlic salt, and heavy cream to an electric mixer. Whip on high speed for 1 minute. Set aside. In another small mixing bowl, combine honey and black pepper. When ready to serve, assemble crostini on a clean work surface. Add a heaping spoonful of whipped ricotta to the toasted crostini. Top with a slice of the spiraled ham and then drizzle with the black pepper honey. **Serves 4**

Chef Adrianne
Liked · 15 hrs

Our Crostini + Whipped Ricotta + Grilled Country Ham + Black Pepper Honey!!!
www.chefadriannes.com

Like · Comment · Share

986 people like this.   Top Comments ▾

34 shares

I "hate" you with all of my stomach! LOL! Diets be damned with your life altering cuisine!
Like · Reply · 👍 1 · 14 hrs

Q rico 😊
See Translation
Like · Reply · 3 hrs

I don't even know what to say about our Nutella Bread Pudding. Just that it should come with a warning Label!

#nutella® and banana sandwich

8 **slices challah bread, or egg bread, 1 inch thick**
½ **cup unsalted butter**
1 **jar, nutella®, chocolate hazelnut spread**
2 **bananas, ripe, sliced**
   sea salt

Heat a large nonstick saute pan over medium heat.

Add butter to melt down.

Meanwhile, spread Nutella® on each of the challah bread slices and sprinkle with sea salt to taste. Top with sliced bananas.

Make four sandwiches out of the eight Nutella® topped challah slices.

Place each sandwich, one at a time, in buttered pan. Cook for 1-2 minutes, or just until warmed through and a crust begins to form. Flip sandwich, and repeat on other side. Repeat steps for all four sandwiches. Enjoy warm. *Serves 4*

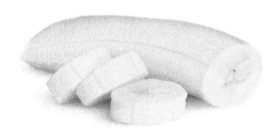

REACHING OUT TO THOSE IN NEED

The unstoppable combination of food, giving, and social media has truly manifested itself in my experiences with St. Jude Research Hospital. The mission that these amazing folks carry out each day is crucial to the improvement and saving of so many children's lives: Assist pediatric cancer patients and their families while constantly working towards wiping out the disease, all without ever charging a penny. St. Jude has been on the front lines of the fight against cancer for over a half century! I am humbled and proud to say that for 7 of those years (and counting), it has provided me with an unforgettable opportunity to both carry on a legacy and receive incredible life lessons in gratitude and the healing power of reaching out to those in need.

I owe my awareness and initial involvement with St. Jude in large part to my sister, who during her own courageous fight against cancer told me how she was driven to emulate a young patient she saw online that was trying to uplift others who were also battling the disease. In a testament to her own beautifully optimistic and giving spirit, she vowed to comfort and counsel others once she conquered her own challenge.

My sister essentially lived by a credo that I credit for steering me in an extremely positive direction in many aspects of my life- "Make It Count". Whatever undertaking we might be involved with- big, small, or in between- her belief was that we should make sure we never looked back on the experience with regret at not having thrown ourselves into it completely. My desire to make sure her spirit and message lived on was the driving force behind me launching the Make It Count Foundation and initially contacting St. Jude in 2007. It's also with that same clarity of purpose that my awesome Chef Adrianne's staff and I pay a yearly visit to the hospital and inevitably come away receiving even more than what we're able to offer.

Our annual December stop at St. Jude stretches several days and really gives us an opportunity to dive in to what is a very social community. Our goal during our stay is to try and bring temporary relief, through the power of food and social contact, to the young patients and their families that reside there. Every year we see what a little social interaction and the power of some good food prepared with a dash of love can do for the strengthening of our connections and bonds to each other.

Sometimes the spark in the children's eyes comes alive simply by associating the aroma of something we might be preparing with the comforting smell of home; on other occasions it's recognizing our faces from one year to the next and feeling that they are not forgotten and are worthy of having special time devoted exclusively to them. And in one particular case, what I initially thought was solely a professional opportunity eventually proved to have much deeper meaning for both myself and the St. Jude community.

Several years ago, I was fortunate to be selected to compete on Food Network's culinary competition show "Chopped". Before the taping of the episode, each participant was asked to designate which individual or charity would be the recipient of the prize money they would be awarded as the winner. Naturally, I had tabbed St. Jude as the potential beneficiary should my dish have captured the top spot. Although I happened to fall short of my ultimate goal on the show, any fears I may have had about having let down my St. Jude "family" were quickly proven way off base! What I was very pleasantly surprised to find was that virtually the entire hospital- patients, caregivers, and staff- had taken a great deal of pride, comfort, and joy in knowing that someone was out there "repping" their cause, and on worldwide TV no less! I even came to find out (and was totally flattered!) by the fact that various "viewing parties" were organized in the St. Jude residences during the different airings of the episode.

Another very personally meaningful experience involved perhaps the most important and truly humbling form of recognition I've ever received in my professional career, which came not from any culinary organization, but from St. Jude itself! In May 2014, I had the incredible honor of receiving a Lifetime Achievement Award from the hospital in acknowledgment of the work that Make It Count has performed on behalf of its patients. To have an effort that began in large part due to the very personal reasons I mentioned earlier be deemed worthy of such a special designation made the moment deeply important. I not only was extremely proud and pleased to see that Make It Count has made a significant difference in the lives of St. Jude patients, I also enjoyed the blessing of feeling a very tangible connection to my sister's legacy at that moment.

Looking back at my history with the hospital, I now realize that this type of unconditional enthusiasm, affection, and appreciation from the St. Jude family is basically

out there "repping" their cause

- #make it count -

the norm. As I mentioned earlier, the hospital boasts an extremely social environment, and its residents and their caregivers really thrive on the strength of social connections to stay upbeat, strong, and positively focused.

In more recent times, social media has also allowed the St. Jude family to gain more widespread attention than ever before. For example, it's been gratifying to see how sometimes one picture of a St. Jude patient with a celebrity visitor generates almost instantaneous interest in the form of plenty of "likes", re-tweets, and positive comments from all over the world. Without a doubt, this always raises the spirit of the child to amazing levels!

Meanwhile, the visibility of Make It Count's involvement with the St. Jude cause has virtually exploded due to channels like Facebook and Twitter. We have been blessed to receive support, inquiries on how to help, and just overall positive vibes from online followers and friends who have felt a connection to what we're striving to do on behalf of St. Jude and other worthy causes that we have been fortunate to be involved with, such as the Make A Wish Foundation, the Susan B. Komen Foundation, and Share Our Strength. Through these same forums we're proud to say we've even applied a little positive "peer pressure" on our followers (many whom, without social media, would be unaware of the need) to contribute whatever they can.

#makeitcount
recipe index

If the filet is the king at Chef Adrianne's, this bone-in Ribeye we call the "cowgirl" is the Queen!

#grilled bone in ribeye
maitre d butter

1 **24 oz bone-in ribeye cut of beef, about 2 ½ inches thick**
¼ **cup extra virgin olive oil**
  kosher salt and freshly ground black pepper
2 **tablespoons unsalted butter, plus 8 addtional table spoons, softened**
1 **cup minced shallots**
  kosher salt
1 **teaspoons ground black pepper**
2 **teaspoons dijon mustard**
½ **teaspoon lemon juice**
2 **tablespoons worcestershire sauce**
½ **parsley, minced**

Season the steak generously with olive oil, salt and pepper. Wrap lightly with plastic wrap and place in the refrigerator for 3-4 hours.

Get the grill to medium high 1 hour before cooking. Remove the steak from the refrigerator and leave at room temperature for the same hour that the grill is getting ready. Allowing the steak to come to room temperature, makes for even cooking. When ready to grill, place the steak on the center of the hot grill and rotate left and right to get proper grill marks. Do this for both sides, about 10 minutes. When this is done, move the steak to a cooler part of the grill and cook to medium rare, 25 to 30 minutes. When ready to serve, top with maître d butter.

MAITRE D BUTTER

In a saute pan, heat 2 tablespoons of the butter over medium heat, then add the shallots. Season with salt, to taste, and cook until they are translucent, about 5 minutes. Transfer the shallots to a medium bowl. Add the black pepper, mustard, lemon juice, and Worcestershire sauce. Whisk to blend so all of the flavors start to meld together. Use a fork to blend in the other 8 tablespoons of butter. Season with salt and pepper, to taste, and stir in the parsley. Roll the butter into a cylinder (like cookie dough) in plastic wrap and refrigerate until ready to use. *Serves 1*

#wild mushroom ravioli
celery brodo, parmesan

1 oz. dried porcini mushrooms, soaked in 1 cup
   boiling water for 25 minutes
½ cup minced shallots
¼ cup extra virgin olive oil
¼ pound fresh wild mushrooms, minced
   kosher salt and freshly ground black pepper
6 garlic cloves, minced
¼ cup dry white wine
1 pound fresh pasta dough sheets
1 pound beef scraps
1 pound beef bones
1 pound pork bones, such as baby back ribs
1 whole chicken, cut into 6 pieces
1 onion, coarsely chopped
1 carrot, coarsely chopped
10 garlic cloves, smashed
7 celery rib, coarsely chopped
10 to 12 quarts cold water
   kosher salt and freshly ground black pepper
1 celery rib, shaved using a potato peeler
½ cup parmesan, freshly grated

Drain the dried mushrooms and mince. In a medium sauté pan, cook the shallots in the olive oil over medium heat, stir. Add the fresh mushrooms and salt and pepper to taste and cook the mixture, stirring, until it is dry. Add the dried mushrooms and the garlic, wine, and cook the mixture, stirring, until it is dry, and transfer it to a bowl.

RAVIOLI:
For the pasta, trim the ends of the dough and cut the dough crosswise into 2 pieces, 1 piece 1 1/2 inches longer than the other. Put a heaping teaspoon of the mushroom mixture in 2 rows on shorter piece, spacing the mixture about 1 inch from the edges and with their centers about 1 1/2 inches apart. Brush the dough around the filling with water, put the longer piece of dough on top, and press it around the mounds of filling. With a fluted pastry wheel, cut the dough between the mounds. Arrange the ravioli in one layer on a baking sheet sprinkled with flour and let dry one hour.

CELERY BRODO:
Place the beef, beef bones, pork bones , chicken pieces, onion, carrot, garlic, and celery in a large soup pot, cover with the water and bring almost to a boil, very slowly. Reduce the heat to

simmer before the mixture boils, and allow to simmer for 4-5 hours, skimming off the foam and any excess fat that rises to the surface with a ladle. After 5 hours, remove from heat, strain the liquid twice, first through a conical sieve and then through a fine cheesecloth, and allow to cool. Refrigerate for up to 1 week or freeze in small batches for up to 1 month.

To serve, ladle hot celery brodo in center of plate. Place mushroom ravioli in brodo and top with freshly grated parmesan cheese. Top with shaved celery. *Serves 4*

#black truffle tagliatelle

½ **pound tagliatelle, freshly made**
4 **tablespoons unsalted butter**
1 **teaspoon garlic, minced**
2 **ounces black truffles, very finely chopped**
1 **cup dry white wine**
¼ **teaspoon freshly grated black pepper**
7 **ounces parmesan cheese, freshly grated**
½ **cup heavy cream**
2 **tablespoons minced fresh chives, for garnish**
 parmesan shavings, for garnish
 kosher salt

Bring a large pot of water to a boil.
Add salt and tagliatelle. Cook until al dente, according to package instructions.
In a medium skillet, melt butter over medium heat. Add garlic, and cook for about 3 minutes. Stir in 1 ounce truffles and a pinch of salt and black pepper.
Cook until tender, 2 to 3 minutes. Add wine and cook until reduced by half, about 5 minutes. Add cheese, and whisk until well incorporated. Stir in remaining 1 ounce truffles. Cook for 2 minutes.
Add the cooked tagliatelle to the sauce and cook for 1-3 minutes or until the sauce begins to coat the pasta. To serve, garnish with chives and parmesan shavings. *Serves 2*

BBQ's, Beer, Funky Beach Chairs,
weekend trips to a small beach town,
Shorts, Movies, and Summer truffles
That's summer alright(

#corvina ceviche
radish, chipotle

2 pounds fresh sea bass or other firm white flesh fish fillets
1 ¼ cups fresh lime juice, divided
½ cup fresh orange juice
½ cup coconut milk
2 jalapeños, seeded and minced
1 red bell pepper, minced
½ red onion, minced
¼ cup cilantro, minced
2 tablespoons radish, thinly sliced
2 tablespoons chopped chives
2 tablespoons extra virgin olive oil sea salt
¼ cup chipotle puree

Cut the fish into 1/2-inch dice and place into a large glass or other nonreactive bowl. Add 1 cup of the lime juice, the orange juice, coconut milk, jalapenos, red bell pepper, and red onion and stir gently to combine. Cover with plastic wrap and refrigerate for at least 6 hours.

To serve the ceviche, pour the liquid off the fish and vegetables and discard liquid.

Toss the fish and vegetables with the remaining lime juice, cilantro, chives, olive oil and salt. Using a cylinder, pack in the ceviche.

Line the top of the cylinder with sliced radishes. Garnish with chipotle and micro greens. *Serves 6*

- #make it count -

One of my good friends, who is
from Peru, once told me, you can't
make a good ceviche without
- Splash of Coconut MILK
milk. or regular

This recipe makes a rich and indulgent lobster seem refreshing and light.

#deconstructed lobster gazpacho
dill, cucumber

2 ½ pounds tomatoes, peeled, roughly chopped
2 red peppers, roughly chopped
2 onions, roughly chopped
2 cucumbers, roughly chopped
4 stalks of celery, roughly chopped
1/3 cup shallots, minced
2 tablespoons garlic, minced
2 tablespoons fresh grated horseradish
¼ cup cilantro, minced
2 cups v-8® juice
2 tablespoons worcestershire sauce
  juice of two lemons
  pinch of cayenne
  kosher salt and freshly ground black pepper
2 pounds cooked lobster, meat
  removed and shells discarded
¼ cup dill, chopped
1 cucumber, sliced length

Using a food processor, combine all the vegetables, shallots, garlic, horseradish, and cilantro together. Puree the mixture until smooth. Add the V-8® juice, Worcestershire sauce and lemon juice and puree again until very smooth. Season with cayenne, salt, and pepper.

Remove and refrigerate for 4-6 hours. To serve, pour some of the tomato mixture onto the bottom of a coupe dish or bowl.

Arrange cooked lobster meat in center of plate. Wrap cucumber slices around finger or end of a wooden spoon to create a cylinder. Arrange, cucumber cylinders around the lobster meat. Top with fresh dill. Enjoy cold. **Serves 4**

To get the gazpacho velvety, silky smooth, I use a high quality super high speed blender.

Fruits and cheeses have been paired for centuries, but fried blueberries and mild gorgonzola are like the odd couple you can't get enough of. LOL!

#grilled new zealand lamb chops
fried blueberries, gorgonzola

2 lbs new zealand lamb chops, frenched
1 tablespoon extra virgin olive oil
1 tablespoon brown sugar
1 teaspoon garlic salt
1 teaspoon freshly ground black pepper
1 teaspoon paprika
½ cup blueberries
½ cup gorgonzola, crumbled
1 cup canola oil, for frying
   chives or micro greens for garnish

Preheat the grill to medium high.

In a small mixing bowl, combine brown sugar, garlic salt, black pepper and paprika. On a work-surface, lay out lamb chops and drizzle with olive oil. Sprinkle lamb chops generously with seasoning mixture.

Allow to sit for 15 minutes. Meanwhile heat at medium sauce pot with canola oil to medium high heat. Once oil is hot, add blueberries and flash fry for 30 seconds.

Place on a paper towel to drain. Place lamb chops on the grill and cook for 3 minutes on each side. Immediately top with gorgonzola while they are still hot so it will allow the cheese to melt a bit. And then finish with fried blueberries and garnishes. **Serves 4**

#toasted gnocchi
parmesan cream, braised beef cheeks

1 cup milk
7 tablespoons unsalted butter
1 teaspoon kosher salt
¾ cup flour
4 eggs
½ cup unsalted butter
1/3 cup all-purpose flour
4 cups milk
¼ teaspoon kosher salt
¼ teaspoon freshly grated black pepper
¾ cup grated parmesan cheese
4 tablespoons extra-virgin olive oil
4 (12-ounce) beef cheeks, trimmed of excess fat
1 yellow onion, chopped
1 carrot, chopped
1 celery rib, chopped
7 garlic cloves, chopped
2 cups red wine
1 (28 ounce) can whole tomatoes , chopped
   including juice
1 ½ teaspoons kosher salt
1 teaspoon freshly ground black pepper
   unsalted butter, for toasting
4 cups baby spinach, washed
½ cup grated parmesan

Combine milk, butter, and ½ teaspoon salt in a medium saucepan.
Bring to a boil over high heat. Add flour and stir with a wooden spoon until mixture is almost solid, about 2-3 minutes. The batter should be the consistency of mashed potatoes and should clear the sides of the pan to form a ball. Remove from heat.
 Pour mixture into the bowl of an electric mixer. Using the paddle attachment on medium speed, add one egg at a time. Meanwhile put a large stockpot of water to simmer.
Fill a pastry bag, fitted with a large plain tip #8, with batter. Holding pastry bag over simmering water, gently squeeze out dough, slicing into 1-inch lengths with a paring knife.
Working in batches of about 20 pieces, cook gnocchi at a slow simmer, stirring occasionally, until they start to puff and float to the top, about 5 minutes.

PARMESAN CREAM:
Melt butter in a medium saucepan over medium-high heat. Whisk in flour, whisking vigorously for 1 minute, gradually adding milk. Bring to a boil, and cook, whisking constantly, 1 to 2 minutes or until thickened. Whisk in Parmesan cheese, salt, and pepper.

BRAISED BEEF CHEEKS:

Preheat the oven to 325 degrees F.

Heat 2 tablespoons oil in a large ovenproof heavy pot over medium high heat until hot but not smoking. While oil is heating, pat beef cheeks dry and season with salt and pepper. Brown beef on all sides, about 20 minutes total, and transfer to a bowl. Pour off fat from pot, then add remaining 2 tablespoons oil and cook onion, carrot, celery, and garlic over medium low heat, stirring until softened, about 10 minutes.

Add wine and scrape up any brown bits. Increase heat to high and boil until liquid is reduced by half, about 10-12 minutes.Return cheeks to pot and add tomatoes with juice, salt, and pepper. Bring to a simmer, then braise, covered, in middle of oven until very tender, about 3 hours.

FOR SERVING:

In a large sauté pan, add a spoonful of butter over high heat. Add cooked gnocchi moving pan around vigorously, not allowing the gnocchi to stick. When gnocchi is golden on all sides, set aside on a paper towel lined plate. In a separate sauté pan, add parmesan cream over medium high heat. Add gnocchi and baby spinach. Place mixture in center of plate. Top with braised beef cheeks and parmesan cheese.

Serves 4

#thecrew

Coincidences? I don't believe in those! It's no coincidence that the very definition of synergy- the creation of a whole that is greater than the simple sum of its parts- consists of essentially the very same words that were once uttered by the wise philosopher I quoted earlier, Aristotle. And "synergy" just so happens to trace its origins to a Greek word that means "working together", the concept that is at the very core of whatever success I've been able to achieve with *Chef Adrianne's*.

When you've been as blessed as I have to constantly have the right people, places, and opportunities work in symphony to enable me to accomplish my dreams, the whole idea of "random chance" gives way to appreciation and trust- trust in those that support you and trust that a singular vision eventually attracts whatever or whomever is needed to fulfill it.

My *Chef Adrianne's* staff-some who have been with me since before Day 1 and the rest who have seamlessly become such an integral part of this incredible journey along the way- are a precious part of the experience we manifest nightly in our corner of Culinary Paradise! Although they truly defy description, the best way I can think of to sum up my feelings and undying appreciation for those that live the dream alongside me daily is this:

To my beloved "crew":
You were completely conscious of the odds stacked against us, yet you all planned forward fearlessly with me; You are both a part of the foundation and of the very bricks that have built up and sustain our wonderfully crazy home away from home; You simultaneously anchor me and elevate me to higher levels; You embody teamwork, yet your priceless individuality brings unparalleled levels of awesomeness to our daily pursuit of perfection; You dive into the push for excellence and live and breathe the quest daily by my side, yet never fail to harness that energy and passion into giving to those less fortunate when the need arises; You refuse to accept even a smidgen of mediocrity, yet you are all beautifully and unapologetically human, capable of mistakes but never allowing them to define or paralyze you; You are tirelessly dedicated and embrace the long hours, yet your talent and commitment make it all seem effortless.

When like-minded and like-energy people fuse their hearts, desire, and dedication, limitations literally crumble! My gratitude for your willingness to demonstrate, day after night and night after day, what the power of working in synergy toward a common vision can accomplish is beyond what I can ever fully express. Thank you for proving that teamwork really does make the dream work!

- #the crew -

219

Mom,

There aren' t any possible words that can fit here. You stood by my side since day 1 when I told you I wanted to be a chef. When everyone was opposed, you supported my decision at 16 years old. It was a moment of impact, pivital to where I stand today. Thank you for showing me everything I know. I like to think that so much of what's good in me comes from you, from my faith in God, to seeing that the only limitations in this world are the ones we set ourselves. You are the strongest person I know. Thank you for traveling the world with me on this crazy adventure, you'll never know what the priviledge of being your daughter means to me. I hope to one day be half of the woman that you are. I love you unconditionally, Molti.

Dad,

My pillar, my foundation, my Dad. You went from making me horrible pig tails and flying saucer sandwiches, to loading up trailers for food and wine festivals. When I look at you, I see love. You have a heart of gold and I cannot thank you enough for your support throughout my whole life. You taught me how to ride bike, and that you don't have to call a repair man for everything. You taught me that people should want more for themselves and I carry that with me everyday. You could have stayed as a welder but became an engineer providing our family with such a great life. Thank you Dad, because I grew up wanting more out of life because of you. You are the example and the reason I push myself everyday. I thank God for having you everyday. I love you, "daddy"

- #the crew -

Raul,

Poo, when I was 15 I'm sorry I told you I wanted to be a physical therapist or a journalist. Two careers of which would have been easier to take than the one I have now. You have stood by my side through culinary school, through all the hard times, and through opening a restaurant in the "middle of nowhere". Thank you for constantly reminding me that you are proud of me and for bringing the greatest joy into my life so far - Coby. My heart is beyond grateful because while we could have been going out and partying, you were satisfied with a few rambunctious nights of craziness a year, and the others were comprised of me working. Thank you for never being that guy who says the wife works too much, instead you've always motivated and supported me. Thank you for filling almost every position in the restaurant when needed, but above all, thank you for years of love you've given me. I will forever be grateful for the nights you came from work straight to massage Yeya's feet because she liked your massages the best. I love you Poo.

Egg,

I've always wanted to share our story. And now I have the platform. Meeting you was serendipity. You came to me through a family friend as I was hiring upon opening the restaurant. You did not want to get hired and you made a phone call to the restaurant because you were put on the spot to inquire about the positions availabe. And I, that never got phone calls, decided to pick up the phone that day. And it was you explaining in vivid detail how you had absolutely no experience. I thought to myself, whoever is crazy enough to say this in an interview is awesome. 7 1/2 years later, here we are...we're still here. Thank you for sharing this incredible journey with me. It has been an honor and a privilege to call you my sous chef and my family. We were just kids: 21 and 22 years old taking on one of the riskiest businesses out there. Thank you for your love and dedication. Thank you for sharing your passion and talent with our guests. I love you.

- #the crew -

Amanda and Nicole,

Girls! You guys have been such a light in my life. What can I say...besides, that it has been an honor to have you represent and be the face of the restaurant in the front of the house. I share my deepest gratitude for every word that you guys have said with enthusiasm and love in our dining room. Words that have touched the dining experience of so many guests. You have been my voice from the kitchen to the dining room. Aside from the privilege of having you on my team, comes the privlege of calling you my friends. Thank you for all the memories we've shared. I still think back sometimes and remember our bowling days. I love you.

Julio (mijo),

Thank you for all you do and all the years of dedication. Thank you for all the laughs, for cracking me up while I've been working nonstop, tirelessly on the line. Thank you for sharing your infamous theories that will forever bring a smile to my face when I think of them. I want you to know that when I see stranged brand energy drinks, I always think of you. But what also makes me think of you is the relentless pursuit of better. Thank you for your dedication. I love you.

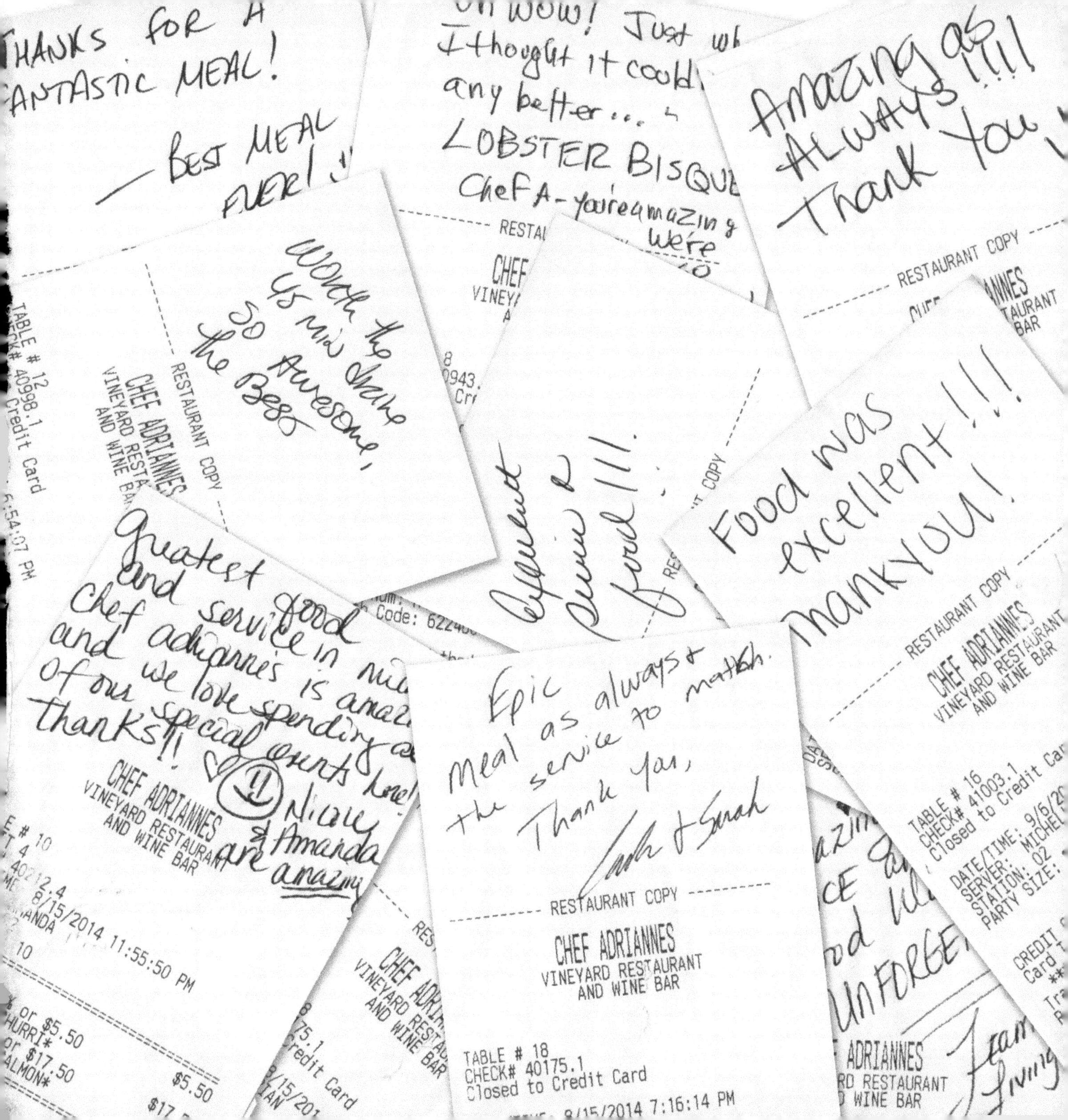

THANKS FOR A
FANTASTIC MEAL!

— BEST MEAL
EVER!

Oh WOW! Just wh
I thought it could
any better... &
LOBSTER BISQUE
Chef A- you're amazing
were

Amazing as
Always!!!!
Thank You

Worth the
us mid drive
So Awesome,
the Best

Food was
excellent!!!!
thankyou!!

Greatest food
and service in mi
Chef Adrianne's is ama
and we love spending a
of our special events here
thanks!! ♡ 😊 Nicole
& Amanda
are amazing

Epic
meal as always &
the service to match.
Thank You,
Jack & Sarah

Printed in the USA
CPSIA information can be obtained
at www.ICGtesting.com
LVHW061541220923
758651LV00014B/890